A Good Read **1**

Developing Strategies for Effective Reading

Book

Carlos Islam
Carrie Steenburgh

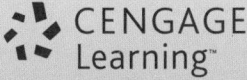

CENGAGE
Learning™

Australia • Brazil • Japan • Korea • Mexico • Singapore • Spain • United Kingdom • United States

A Good Read 1:
Developing Strategies for
Effective Reading
Student Book

Carlos Islam
Carrie Steenburgh

Publishing Director:
Paul Tan

Senior Product Manager:
Michael Cahill

Editor:
Andrew Jessop

Senior Publishing Executive:
Gemaine Goh

Illustrator:
Ng Huk Keng

Designer:
Redbean De Pte Ltd

Cover Images:
Getty Images Sales
Singapore Pte Ltd

ISBN-13: 978-981-4246-95-8

ISBN-10: 981-4246-95-6

Cengage Learning Asia Pte Ltd
5 Shenton Way #01-01
UIC Building
Singapore 068808

Cengage Learning is a leading provider of customized learning solutions with office locations around the globe, including Singapore, the United Kingdom, Australia, Mexico, Brazil and Japan.

Locate your local office at: **www.cengage.com/global**

Cengage Learning products are represented in Canada by Nelson Education, Ltd.

For product information, visit **www.cengageasia.com**

The publisher would like to thank the following for their permission to reproduce photographs on the following pages:

© 2008 Jupiterimages Corporation: 27, 45, 49, 53, 61, 67, 69, 75, 77, 89, 92, 95, 97, 107, 109, 111.
© 2008 Shutterstock Images LLC: 09, 13, 17, 19, 27, 39, 41, 105.
© 2008 Getty Images Sales Singapore Pte Ltd: Cover, 09, 33, 47, 85.

Please note that all people shown are models and are used only for illustrative purposes.

Printed in Singapore
2 3 4 5   11 10 09 08

Dedication and Acknowledgements

We owe a great debt of gratitude to Chris Sol Cruz, Sean Bermingham and Ian Purdon at Cengage Learning. This project owes its life and direction to Chris' initial trust and backing. Sean has steered us through our growing pains while Ian has held our hand nurturing *A Good Read* with his invaluable insights and suggestions.

We thank all the students at Union County College who piloted much of the material in this series and whose feedback has been crucial.

We'd also like to thank our parents for giving us our lives and our characters.

We dedicate this book to Cecelia and Anna.

The publisher would also like to thank the following people for their assistance in developing this series:

Chiou-lan Chern, National Taiwan Normal University
Nancy Garcia, Riverbank High School
Brian Heldenbrand, Jeonju University
Kristin Johannsen
Kevin Knight, Kanda Gaigo Career College
Debra J Martinez
Ahmed M. Motala, University of Sharjah
Tufi Neder Neto, Colégio Loyola
Chris Ruddenklau, Kinki University
Scott Smith, Hongik University
Vilma Sousa, Colégio Rio Branco
Naowarat Tongkam, Silpakorn University
Nobuo Tsuda, Konan University
Cally Williams, Newcomers High School
Young Hee Cheri Lee, Reading Town USA English Language Institute
Zainor Izat Zainal, Universiti Putra Malaysia
Vilma Zapata, Miami-Dade County Public Schools

Contents

Welcome to A Good Read

To the Student:

Reading is a very important part of language learning. Studies show that the more you read, the more you will improve your general English language ability. Through reading, you will build your vocabulary, increase your understanding of grammar, and improve your writing.

In this book, you will find:
- interesting texts, on topics such as personality, life-changing moments, and urban legends.
- simple explanations of reading strategies (ways you can read a text to help understanding), and activities to help you practice these strategies.
- activities to help you recognize and understand word chunks (words that go together, for example, "black and white," "fast car," "spend time") that will help develop your vocabulary.

By practicing reading strategies and learning word chunks, you will become a much better reader: You will be able to understand more and enjoy more of what you read.

Carrie and Carlos

To the Teacher:

What do students really need to help them become better readers of English?

A Good Read is designed to help your students become better readers by presenting and practicing reading strategies more explicitly and deliberately than other reading series. These strategies range from core reading techniques—such as skimming and scanning, through "guessing" strategies—such as inferring and predicting, to "personal or reflective" strategies—such as visualizing and summarizing. By learning and practicing these strategies, your students will be able to read more naturally, effectively, and fluently.

In addition, Word Work activities accompanying each reading have been included to encourage your students to recognize and understand word chunks (groups of words that are frequently found together in texts). Examples of word chunks are "black and white," "leave home," and "first of all." Experts[1] suggest that noticing word chunks improves reading as well as other language skills, as students remember language as whole chunks, not individual words. This saves the reader time and mental energy when reading so that they become more fluent and effective readers.

Carrie and Carlos

---

[1] Lewis, M., 1993, The Lexical Approach, Hove: Language Teaching Publications

Key Features

Start thinking about the unit topic and related language.

Learn how to use the unit's reading strategy.

Try some practice activities.

Read the feedback to check your answers and understanding of the strategy.

Think about the reading and related language.

Complete authentic while reading tasks.

Practice reading strategies covered earlier.

Reflect on the reading and do the activities to check comprehension.

The book contains four review units.

Use the vocabulary index on pages 120 - 127 to help understand unfamiliar words.

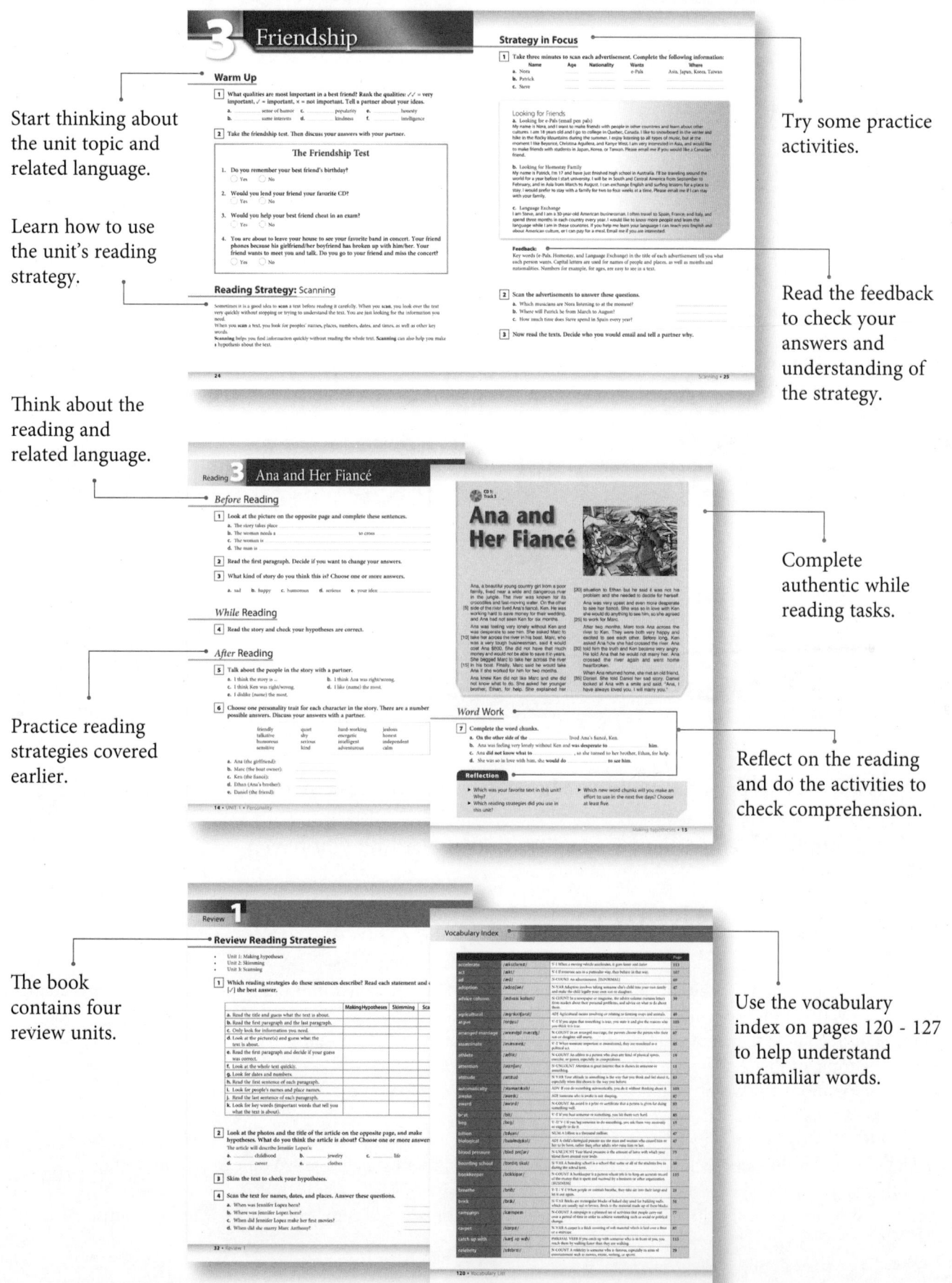

1 Personality

Warm Up

1 Each adjective in the box describes a personality trait. Match one with each picture.

Personality Traits

hard-working	intelligent	energetic/active	serious
humorous/funny	outgoing/friendly	shy/quiet	calm
kind/caring	honest sensitive	creative	adventurous

A _____

B _____

C _____

D _____

E _____

F _____

2 What type of personality do you have? Circle your three main personality traits.

3 Ask other students what personality traits they think you have.

Reading Strategy: Making hypotheses (Guessing)

Good readers make guesses about the text before they read. This is called **making hypotheses**. They also change their guesses (hypotheses) while they are reading.

Before you read a text, look at the title, the headings, and pictures. Then make hypotheses about:

- the topic of the text
- the opinions the writer will have
- the words the text will use
- how the text will make you feel

While you read, you can check your hypotheses and change them if necessary. You can also make new hypotheses.

This reading strategy will help you understand more as you read, and remember more when you finish reading.

Strategy in Focus

1 Look at the title and photos. What do you think the article is about? Choose the best answer.

  a. The unusual personality traits of these famous people
  b. How these famous people celebrate their birthdays
  c. The typical personalities of people born under these star signs

Personality and Star Sign

Gwen Stefani: born 3 October 1969, star sign = Libra

The singer Gwen Stefani is a Libran. People born under this sign are usually outgoing and enjoy working with other people. They are usually creative and attractive. People born under the Libra sign are usually happy and sensitive.

Libra

2 Read the first and second sentence of the above text. Decide if you want to change your hypothesis.

Feedback:

The best answer is c. Some people in the West believe that your star sign influences your personality.

3 Look at the title of the following texts. What do you think they will be about? Choose the best answer.

  a. the personality traits of people born under the Aquarius and Cancer star signs
  b. the personal traits of Oprah Winfrey and Lindsay Lohan
  c. the life of Oprah Winfrey and Lindsay Lohan

Oprah Winfrey: born 29 January 1954, star sign = Aquarius

The TV talk-show host Oprah Winfrey is an Aquarius. People born under this sign are usually intelligent and honest. People born under this sign also care about other people very much. They think it is important that everyone is treated fairly.

Aquarius

Lindsay Lohan: born 2 July 1986, star sign = Cancer

The actress Lindsay Lohan was born under the sign of Cancer. These people are usually very sensitive. They don't hide their feelings so it is easy to see if they are happy, sad, or angry. If you were born under this sign, you are probably very kind and like to have very close friends.

Cancer

Feedback:

The correct answer is a. These two texts clearly come from the article *Personality and Star Sign*, as the texts contain similar information. Also, the words "Aquarius" and "Cancer", other Western star signs, appear in the headings.

Birth Order and Personality

Before Reading

1 Look at the title of the text and the picture. What do you think the text is about? Choose the best answer (make a hypothesis).

　a. The time you were born and your personality.

　b. The personality traits of the eldest, and youngest child in a family.

　c. The personality traits of boys and girls.

2 Read the first sentence of each paragraph to check your hypothesis. Decide if you want to change your answer (your hypothesis).

3 What do you think the text will say about birth order and personality? Circle the answers you think are correct.

　a. The first-born child is:　　　outgoing / hard-working / creative.

　b. The second child is:　　　　outgoing / hard-working / creative.

　c. The youngest child is:　　　outgoing / hard-working / creative.

While Reading

4 As you read the text, check your answers (hypotheses).

After Reading

5 Ask a partner the following questions.

　a. Do you have any brothers or sisters? If so, are you a first-born, second-born, or younger child?

　b. Do you believe that birth order can influence your personality?

6 Decide if the statements are true (**T**) or false (**F**), according to the text.

　a.　**T**　**F**　Brothers and sisters usually have the same personalities.

　b.　**T**　**F**　A lot of successful people are first-born children.

　c.　**T**　**F**　It is difficult for the second child to get his or her parents' attention.

　d.　**T**　**F**　The second child is very similar to the first-born child.

　e.　**T**　**F**　The youngest child tends to be creative.

　f.　**T**　**F**　The youngest child learns to be responsible from a young age.

CD 1:
Track 1

Birth Order and Personality

If you have a brother or sister, you already know you are different from each other. You live together in the same house and have the same parents, but you have different personalities. [5] Why is this? One possible reason is the way your parents treat you.

First-born children receive all the attention from their parents. Most families have twice as many photos of a first-born than any other child. [10] Parents tend to give first-borns more responsibility and depend on them to take care of younger brothers and sisters. As a result, first-borns are often responsible, hard-working, and serious. They often want to do well at school and work. [15] There are more first-born American Presidents— for example George W. Bush, George Washington, and Lyndon Baines Johnson—than second or last-born children.

When a second child arrives, parents are more [20] relaxed. The second child is allowed to be more independent, but also has to compete with the first-born for the parents' attention and love. These children often choose different sports and hobbies to show independence and they develop [25] different personality traits. They are often adventurous, fun-loving, and outgoing, but can be jealous and get angry easily.

The youngest child tends to be the happiest, and has fewer responsibilities and more freedom. [30] These children do not feel pressure to do well at school and work, but have to be creative to get their family's attention. They are often friendly, humorous, and calm. Many famous talk-show hosts and comedians were born [35] last.

Word Work

7 **Complete the sentences using the word chunks below.**

> brothers and sisters   want to do well   fun-loving   as a result   depend on

a. Everyone in my class has been studying hard. We all _____ in the English test.

b. Ken joined the English club at school and _____ has made a lot of new friends.

c. Sue likes to go to parties, meet new people and enjoy herself. She is a real _____ girl.

d. My friend Aya doesn't have any_____. She is an only child.

e. Young children _____ their parents for love and affection.

Before Reading

1 How do you make a hypothesis? Circle the statements you think are correct.

a. Read and understand every word in the text.
b. Read the title and guess what the text is about.
c. Look at the pictures and guess what the text is about.
d. Read the first paragraph and decide if your guess was correct.
e. Look at the whole text quickly and guess what it is about.

2 Look at the title of the text on the opposite page. What do you think the text is about? (Make a hypothesis.) Choose the best answer.

a. How listening to music changes your personality.
b. How you choose music according to your mood.
c. How your taste in music can identify your personality.
d. How people copy the personality traits of their favorite musicians.

While Reading

3 Read the first paragraph of the text. Then decide if you want to change your answer to one of the following:

a. A married couple called Jim and Sue.
b. A punk rock band called the New York Dolls.
c. How listening to music changes your personality.
d. How you choose music according to your mood.
e. How your taste in music can identify your personality.

4 Continue reading the text and check your hypothesis.

After Reading

5 Decide if these statements are true (**T**) or false (**F**), according to the text.

a. **T** **F** Sue and Jim dated for five years before they got married.
b. **T** **F** You can tell more about people from their clothes than their taste in music.
c. **T** **F** Fans of classical music are shy and fans of rap are quiet.
d. **T** **F** People who like the same type of music often have similar personality traits.

6 Read the text again. Find the personality traits for each type of music:

a. punk rock _____
b. rock and pop _____
c. heavy metal / rap _____
d. classical _____
e. jazz _____
f. hip-hop _____

CD 1:
Track 2

Your Music and Your Personality

Sue and Jim were neighbors for five years but they were never interested in each other. Then one day, Sue saw Jim's music collection. She noticed a rare punk rock CD that she also owned. [5] At that moment, she realized that they both shared the same interest in music and they started talking. Sue said, "I thought we had nothing in common until I saw his CD by the New York Dolls." They are now married and living with each other.

[10] Some psychologists believe that your taste in music is related to your personality. As part of a test at the University of Texas, Austin, USA, volunteers created a CD of their favorite songs. The volunteers then listened to each other's CDs [15] and made guesses about the CD creator's personality—outgoing, adventurous, happy, and so on. These strangers correctly guessed much more about each others' personalities through their CDs than through their clothes or taste in [20] films. For example, Sue and Jim love punk music, which means they have outgoing personalities.

The psychologists who carried out the test found Snoop Dogg (hip-hop) fans are likely to be energetic and talkative. People who like U2 [25] (rock/pop music) are generally independent and adventurous.

The psychologists also found that Louis Armstrong (jazz) fans tend to be serious and [30] intelligent while fans of classical music are also likely to enjoy jazz music and tend to be shy. The psychologists were surprised to find that rap and heavy metal fans were also shier and quieter than many other music lovers.

Word Work

7 Correct the mistakes in these word chunks, without looking at the text.

a. Sue and Jim were neighbors for five years, but they were never **interested in some other**.

_____

b. She realized that they both **shared the same hobby in music** and they started talking.

_____

c. "I thought we had **nothing in similar** until I saw a CD by the New York Dolls."

_____

d. Sue and Jim are now **married and living each other**.

_____

Ana and Her Fiancé

Before Reading

1 Look at the picture on the opposite page and complete these sentences.

 a. The story takes place _____ .
 b. The woman needs a _____ to cross _____ .
 c. The woman is _____ .
 d. The man is _____ .

2 Read the first paragraph. Decide if you want to change your answers.

3 What kind of story do you think this is? Choose one or more answers.

 a. sad b. happy c. humorous d. serious e. your idea: _____

While Reading

4 Read the story and check your hypotheses are correct.

After Reading

5 Talk about the people in the story with a partner.

 a. I think the story is ... b. I think Ana was right/wrong.
 c. I think Ken was right/wrong. d. I like (name) the most.
 e. I dislike (name) the most.

6 Choose one personality trait for each character in the story. There are a number of possible answers. Discuss your answers with a partner.

friendly	quiet	hard-working	jealous
talkative	shy	energetic	honest
humorous	serious	intelligent	independent
sensitive	kind	adventurous	calm

 a. Ana (the girlfriend): _____
 b. Marc (the boat owner): _____
 c. Ken (the fiancé): _____
 d. Ethan (Ana's brother): _____
 e. Daniel (the friend): _____

CD 1:
Track 3

Ana and Her Fiancé

Ana, a beautiful young country girl from a poor family, lived near a wide and dangerous river in the jungle. The river was known for its crocodiles and fast-moving water. On the other [5] side of the river lived Ana's fiancé, Ken. He was working hard to save money for their wedding, and Ana had not seen Ken for six months.

Ana was feeling very lonely without Ken and was desperate to see him. She asked Marc to [10] take her across the river in his boat. Marc, who was a very tough businessman, said it would cost Ana $800. She did not have that much money and would not be able to save it in years. She begged Marc to take her across the river [15] in his boat. Finally, Marc said he would take Ana if she worked for him for two months.

Ana knew Ken did not like Marc and she did not know what to do. She asked her younger brother, Ethan, for help. She explained her [20] situation to Ethan but he said it was not his problem and she needed to decide for herself.

Ana was very upset and even more desperate to see her fiancé. She was so in love with Ken she would do anything to see him, so she agreed [25] to work for Marc.

After two months, Marc took Ana across the river to Ken. They were both very happy and excited to see each other. Before long, Ken asked Ana how she had crossed the river. Ana [30] told him the truth and Ken became very angry. He told Ana that he would not marry her. Ana crossed the river again and went home heartbroken.

When Ana returned home, she met an old friend, [35] Daniel. She told Daniel her sad story. Daniel looked at Ana with a smile and said, "Ana, I have always loved you. I will marry you."

Word Work

7 **Complete the word chunks.**

a. **On the other side of the** _____ lived Ana's fiancé, Ken.

b. Ana was feeling very lonely without Ken and **was desperate to** _____ **him**.

c. Ana **did not know what to** _____ , so she turned to her brother, Ethan, for help.

d. She was so in love with him, she **would do** _____ **to see him**.

Reflection

▶ Which was your favorite text in this unit? Why?

▶ Which reading strategies did you use in this unit?

▶ Which new word chunks will you make an effort to use in the next five days? Choose at least five.

2 Happiness

Warm Up

How happy are you? Take the happiness test. Then score your answers.

Are You Happy?

1. **When your teacher gives you a leaflet, you:**
   a. say thank you.
   b. nod your head.
   c. say nothing.

2. **How often do you send instant messages (IM)?**
   a. never.
   b. sometimes.
   c. all the time.

3. **When shopping for a new cell phone, you:**
   a. buy it right away.
   b. wait and think about it.
   c. look for the best deal.

4. **You would rather buy:**
   a. a bike, a skateboard, or ticket to a game/concert.
   b. a TV, video game, or stereo.
   c. an expensive watch, jewelry, or designer clothes.

Give yourself 3 points for every a, 2 points for every b and 1 point for every c.
9–12 points: You have the secret of happiness—please share!
5–8 points: You probably have good and bad days but you are probably happy.
1–4 points: You tend to feel blue.

Feedback:
1. Saying "thank you" is a quick and easy way to develop relationships.
2. According to studies, people who talk with their friends on the phone or in person are happier than people who depend on IM to communicate.
3. Unhappy people often find it difficult to make decisions.
4. Spending money on experiences makes people happier than buying goods, such as watches, clothes, and jewelry.

Reading Strategy: Skimming

Good readers usually look at a text quickly before they start reading carefully. This is called skimming.
You can skim a text in different ways. You can read:
- the title and other headings, and look at the pictures.
- the first sentence of each paragraph.
- the last sentence of each paragraph.
- the first and last paragraph.

If you do not have time to read the text carefully, you can use several skimming methods to understand it. Skimming helps you understand the main idea of the text before reading it carefully. It helps you make and check your hypothesis. Skimming can also help you decide if you need or want to read the whole text.

Strategy in Focus

1 Take one minute to skim the text. Look at the title, the pictures, and read the first sentence of each paragraph. What is the main idea of the text?

a. Money doesn't make you happy.
b. Advice to make yourself happier.
c. Ideas for helping other people to be happy.

The Secrets of Happiness

Most people want to be happy, but few know how to find happiness. Money and success alone do not bring lasting happiness. Aristotle, a Greek philosopher, said, "Happiness depends upon ourselves." In other words, we make our own happiness. Here are a few suggestions to help you be happier.

The first secret of happiness is to enjoy the simple things in life. Too often, we spend so much time thinking about the future—for example, getting into college or getting a good job—that we fail to enjoy the present. You should enjoy life's simple pleasures, such as reading a good book, listening to your favorite music, or spending time with close friends. People who have several close friends tend to live happier and healthier lives.

Another secret to leading a happy life is to be active, and have hobbies where you forget your problems and lose track of time. Many people experience this dancing, or playing a sport, such as snowboarding or soccer. You can forget about your problems, and only think about the activity.

Finally, many people find happiness in helping others. According to studies, people feel good when they volunteer their time to help others. If you want to feel happier, do something nice for someone. You can help a friend with his or her studies, go shopping to buy food for an elderly relative, or simply help out around the house by washing the dishes.

2 Read the text more carefully and decide if you were correct about its main idea.

Feedback:

The best answer is b. as the text gives many suggestions on how the reader can find happiness. Answers a. and c. are mentioned only as examples.

Just a Game?

Before Reading

1 Take two minutes to skim the text. Look at the title, the pictures, and read the first and last sentence of each paragraph. What is the main idea of the text?

   a. Sam Russell is not a healthy person.

   b. Sports fans are generally happy people.

   c. Sports fans are only happy when their team wins.

While Reading

2 Read the text more carefully and check your hypothesis. Underline the sentences that support your hypothesis.

After Reading

3 Ask a partner these questions about the text.

   a. What is the main idea of the text?

   b. What do you think of Sam Russell?

4 Find these words in the text. Underline your answers in the text.

   a. What does the word "this" in line 8 refer to?

   b. What do the words "their" in line 16 and line 17 refer to?

   c. What does the word "those" in line 22 refer to?

   d. What does the word "that" in line 28 refer to?

5 Decide if the statements are true (T) or false (F), according to the text.

a.	T	F	Sam Russell does not like the Boston Red Sox.
b.	T	F	Sam Russell changes his work and social events to watch the Red Sox.
c.	T	F	One study found that it is healthy to be a sports fan.
d.	T	F	A sports fan whose team loses a lot is always depressed.
e.	T	F	Although he has lost some friends, being a Red Sox fan has made Sam Russell happy.

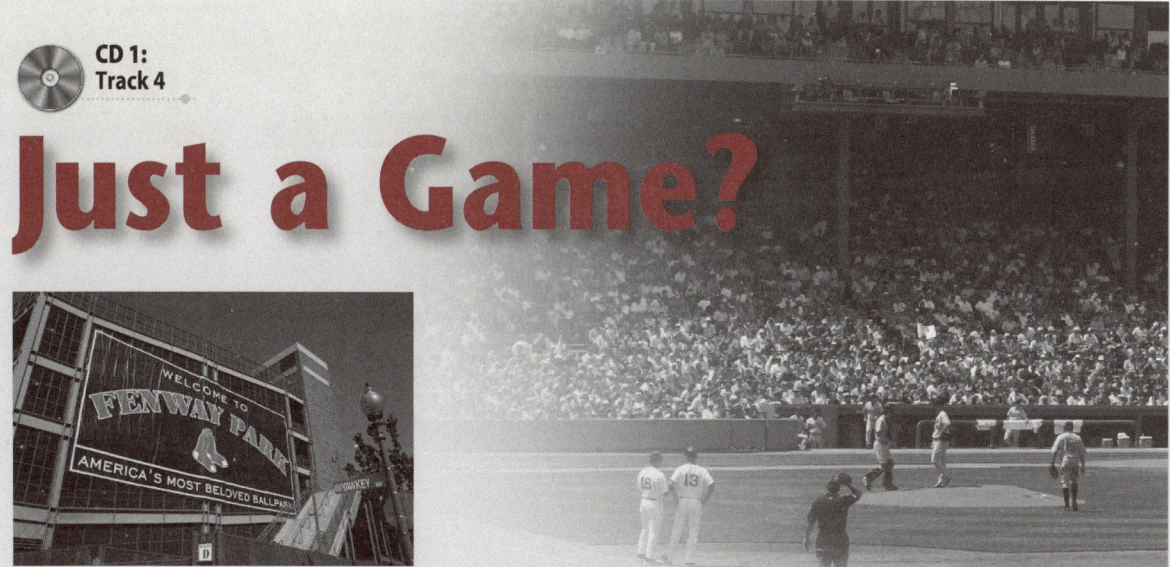

CD 1:
Track 4

Just a Game?

Sam Russell is not your average baseball fan. He is a die-hard Boston Red Sox fan. He has a season ticket and he arranges his work schedule so he does not miss a game. Sam [5] also attends games dressed in their uniform, and his car is red. He has even lost some friends by choosing to watch the Red Sox instead of going to their weddings. Is this healthy behavior?

[10] Although Russell's case is extreme, being a sports fan can be healthy for you. According to a study at the University of Kansas in the USA, sports fans suffer from depression less than people who are not interested in sports. [15] Sports fans also experience other effects from watching their team play. When their team wins a game, their own confidence and happiness increase, just like the athletes. Losing, on the other hand, always leads to [20] some sense of disappointment.

What about die-hard fans whose team always loses? The team spirit keeps those fans from losing hope. Knowing that other fans are probably feeling the same way also helps them. [25] In addition, there is always the hope that their team will win the next game. Russell has lost some friends because of his love for baseball and although you may think that would make him unhappy, he has made many more new [30] friends because of his team spirit.

For Sam Russell, supporting the Red Sox is not just a hobby; it is a way of life and the secret to his happiness.

Word Work

6 Rewrite the sentences using the word chunks below. Then look at the text to check your answers.

on the other hand,	arranges his work schedule	in addition,
a die-hard ... fan	instead of going	

a. Sam Russell is a big Boston Red Sox supporter.

_____

b. He organizes his calendar so he does not miss a game.

_____

c. He has even lost some friends by choosing to watch the Red Sox rather than go to their weddings.

_____

d. However, losing a game always leads to some sense of disappointment.

_____

e. Furthermore, there is always the hope that their team will win the next game.

_____

Laughter Really is the Best Medicine

Before Reading

1 Decide how to skim a text. Choose the statements you think are correct.

a. Read the title.
b. Discuss the title with a friend.
c. Look at the picture.
d. Read every word in the text from start to finish.
e. Read the first paragraph and the last paragraph.
f. Read the first sentence of each paragraph.
g. Read the last sentence of each paragraph.
h. Look at the whole text quickly.

2 Take two minutes to skim the text. What is the main idea of the text?

a. Laughter clubs can be good for your health.
b. Everyone should tell a joke once a day.
c. Laughter clubs help people with heart problems.
d. Dr. Mandan Kataria created the world's first laughter club.

While Reading

3 As you read the text, check your hypothesis. Then decide if this type of club would be popular in your country.

After Reading

4 Ask a partner these questions about the text.

a. Do you think they would be popular in our/your country?
b. Would you join a laughter club? Why? / Why not?

5 Choose the correct ending to complete the statements.

a. According to the article, people who laugh:
   i. watch movies all the time.   **ii.** have more friends   **iii.** have a healthier life.
b. The highest number of laughter clubs is found in:
   i. the United States.   **ii.** India.   **iii.** Korea.
c. At a laughter club meeting, people:
   i. listen to jokes.   **ii.** watch funny movies.   **iii.** do laughing exercises.
d. Laughter clubs are popular in:
   i. hospitals and nursing homes.   **ii.** high schools.   **iii.** banks.

CD 1: Track 5

Laughter Really is the Best Medicine

In a study at the University of Maryland Medical Center in Baltimore, researchers found that people who had a good sense of humor and [5] laughed a lot had fewer heart problems than people who laughed less.

After reading about the benefits of laughing, a doctor in India decided [10] to start a laughter club. Dr. Mandan Kataria's laughter club quickly grew into 1,800 groups throughout India and over 6,000 around the world. The laughter club has even inspired a World [15] Laughter Day, which people celebrate on the first Sunday of May.

Instructors at the clubs get people laughing not through jokes but through simple laughing exercises. For [20] example, instructors and participants repeat the chant "ho-ho-ho-ha-ha-ha" together. Participants also do the Lion Laugh by sticking out their tongues and waving their hands around their ears. Other exercises focus [25] on breathing and simple yoga exercises.

These laughter clubs are very popular in hospitals and nursing homes, where participants can forget about their aches and pains while laughing. It seems that laughing may be just as important [30] as eating right and exercising.

How can you make laughing a part of your daily routine? If you feel funny about joining a laughter club, you can rent a funny movie, remember a funny experience, do some sports, or go to the [35] zoo and watch the monkeys. You will not be able to keep a straight face.

So, don't worry, be happy—laugh a little and live longer.

Word Work

7 Correct the mistakes in these word chunks, without looking at the text.

a. People who **had a good feeling of humor** and laughed a lot had fewer heart problems.

_____

b. Dr. Mandan Kataria's laughter club quickly grew into 1,800 groups throughout India and over 6,000 **around the earth**. _____

c. Other exercises **focus it** breathing and simple yoga stretches. _____

d. Participants can forget about their **aches and injuries** while laughing. _____

e. How can you make laughing a part of your **daily habit**? _____

Before Reading

1 Take two minutes to skim the story *A Businessman's View*. What is the story about?

   a. A businessman learns how to fish.
   b. A fisherman wants to become a businessman.
   c. A businessman gives advice to a fisherman.

2 Tell a partner what you think the main idea of the story is.

While Reading

3 Read the story more carefully and check your hypothesis.

After Reading

4 Ask a partner these questions about the text.

   a. What do you think makes the American businessman happy?
   b. What do you think makes the Mexican fisherman happy?
   c. What is a "full and busy life" (paragraph 7) for the businessman, the fisherman, and for you?

5 Rewrite these sentences so that they are true for the story.

   a. Martin had been going on vacation to the fishing village for a couple of years.

   _____

   b. It took Pablo all day to catch the fish.

   _____

   c. Pablo thinks his life is too busy.

   _____

   d. Martin thinks Pablo can make more money by buying a supermarket.

   _____

   e. When Pablo retires as a millionaire, his lifestyle will be very different.

   _____

A Businessman's View

[1] Martin Lynch, an American businessman, had been going on vacation to a small Mexican fishing village for a number of years. One morning while going for a walk along the beach, he saw his friend Pablo Perez, a local fisherman. Martin watched Pablo unload his boat and pack the fish in a box.

[2] Martin noticed Pablo was smiling and looked very happy. He could also see several large fish in the boat. Martin greeted Pablo and asked how long it took to catch the fish.

[3] "Just a few hours," replied Pablo.

[4] Martin asked, "Why didn't you stay longer and catch more fish."

[5] "I have enough for my family," Pablo said.

[6] "And what do you do with the rest of your day?" asked Martin.

[7] "I take a nap, play with my children, spend time with my wife, and go into the village to see my friends and play cards. I have a full and busy life."

[8] Martin explained that if Pablo worked longer hours and caught more fish, he could make more money. With the extra money, Pablo could buy more boats and catch many more fish. By selling the fish, Pablo could open his own factory and sell direct to supermarkets.

[9] "Then what?" asked Pablo.

[10] "Well you would probably have to move to Mexico City to run the business. Eventually, you would be able to sell your business and make millions of dollars," replied Martin.

[11] "How long will that take?" asked Pablo.

[12] Martin thought for a while and said it would probably take at least 15 years.

[13] "And then what?" asked Pablo.

[14] "Well, that's the best part," Martin said. "You will be able to retire, buy a house near the ocean, sleep longer, play with your children, spend more time with your wife, see your friends, and play cards."

Word Work

6 Complete the word chunks using the verbs in the box. You can use some of the verbs more than once.

run	stay	go	spend	catch	make	take

a. _____ on vacation

b. _____ for a walk

c. _____ the fish

d. _____ longer

e. _____ the business

f. _____ more money

g. _____ time with

h. _____ a nap

Reflection

▶ Which was your favorite text in this unit? Why?

▶ Which reading strategies did you use in this unit?

▶ Which new word chunks will you make an effort to use in the next five days? Choose at least five.

3 Friendship

Warm Up

1 What qualities are most important in a best friend? Rank the qualities: √√ = very important, √ = important, × = not important. Tell a partner about your ideas.

a. _____ sense of humor　　b. _____ same interests　　c. _____ popularity

d. _____ kindness　　e. _____ honesty　　f. _____ intelligence.

2 Take the friendship test. Then discuss your answers with your partner.

The Friendship Test

1. Do you remember your best friend's birthday?
   ◯ Yes　　◯ No

2. Would you lend your friend your favorite CD?
   ◯ Yes　　◯ No

3. Would you help your best friend cheat in an exam?
   ◯ Yes　　◯ No

4. You are about to leave your house to see your favorite band in concert. Your friend phones because his girlfriend/her boyfriend has broken up with him/her. Your friend wants to meet you and talk. Do you go to your friend and miss the concert?
   ◯ Yes　　◯ No

Reading Strategy: Scanning

Sometimes it is a good idea to **scan** a text before reading it carefully. When you **scan**, you look over the text very quickly without stopping or trying to understand the text. You are just looking for the information you need.

When you **scan** a text, you look for peoples' names, places, numbers, dates, and times, as well as other key words.

Scanning helps you find information quickly without reading the whole text. **Scanning** can also help you make a hypothesis about the text.

Strategy in Focus

1 Take three minutes to scan each advertisement. Complete the following information:

Name	Age	Nationality	Wants	Where
a. Nora	_____	_____	e-Pals	Asia, Japan, Korea, Taiwan
b. Patrick	_____	_____	_____	_____
c. Steve	_____	_____	_____	_____

Looking for Friends

a. Looking for e-Pals (email pen pals)
My name is Nora, and I want to make friends with people in other countries and learn about other cultures. I am 18 years old and I go to college in Quebec, Canada. I like to snowboard in the winter and hike in the Rocky Mountains during the summer. I enjoy listening to all types of music, but at the moment I like Beyoncé, Christina Aguilera, and Kanye West. I am very interested in Asia, and would like to make friends with students in Japan, Korea, or Taiwan. Please email me if you would like a Canadian e-pal.

b. Looking for Homestay Family
My name is Patrick, I'm 17 and have just finished high school in Australia. I'll be traveling around the world for a year before I start university. I will be in South and Central America from September to February, and in Asia from March to August. I can exchange English and surfing lessons for a place to stay. I would prefer to stay with a family for two to four weeks at a time. Please email me if I can stay with your family.

c. Language Exchange
I am Steve, and I am a 30-year-old American businessman. I often travel to Spain, France, and Italy, and spend three months in each country every year. I would like to know more people and learn the language while I am in these countries. If you help me learn your language I can teach you English and about American culture, or I can pay for a meal. Email me if you are interested.

Feedback:
Key words (e-Pals, Homestay, and Language Exchange) in the title of each advertisement tell you what each person wants. Capital letters are used for names of people and places, as well as months and nationalities. Numbers for example, for ages, are easy to see in a text.

2 Scan the advertisements to answer these questions.

a. Which musicians are Nora listening to at the moment? _____

b. Where will Patrick be from March to August? _____

c. How much time does Steve spend in Spain every year? _____

3 Now read the texts. Decide who you would email and tell a partner why.

What I like Most About My Best Friend

Before Reading

1 Scan the texts to complete the information below.

	Name	Nationality	Best Friend's Name	Best Friend's Personality Traits
a.	Lilly Chen	_____	_____	_____
b.	Alan Cordoba	_____	_____	_____
c.	Isabel Famosa	_____	_____	_____
d.	Ken Ichigawa	_____	_____	_____

While Reading

2 As you read the text, underline any statements that are true for you and your best friend.

After Reading

3 Ask a partner these questions about the text.

a. Whose best friend do you like most? Why?

b. What personality traits do you like most?

4 Decide if the statements are true (T) or false (F), according to the text.

a. T F May and Lilly are good friends because they have similar personalities.

b. T F Fanny is a caring person.

c. T F Isabel and Ana both live in Cuba.

d. T F Ken doesn't like Daisuke's jokes.

5 Circle the adjective that is NOT true for each best friend.

a.	May is:	confident	outgoing	shy
b.	Fanny is:	intelligent	calm	interesting
c.	Ana is:	serious	honest	kind
d.	Daisuke is:	funny	quiet	talkative

CD 1:
Track 7

What I Like Most About My Best Friend

Lilly Chen, Taiwan

May is the most confident girl that I have ever met. Although she looks tough, she is really kind. It may surprise some people to find out that May and I are best friends, because we have very different personalities. I lack confidence and I am quite shy, which is the opposite of May but I think this is why we are such good friends.

Isabel Famosa, Cuba

My best friend is Ana Hernandez. She is honest, kind, and sensitive. We were born in the same city in Cuba. We spent a lot of time together until we were 12. Then, I moved to America with my family and I thought I would never see Ana again. When I went to college in New York, Ana had a room in the same dormitory. She now lives near me in New Jersey and we see each other all the time.

Alan Cordoba, Mexico

My best friend is Fanny, my girlfriend. I can always depend on her. We always take care of each other. The first week we met, I got sick with flu and she came to my house to take care of me every day. She is also very intelligent and interesting, although sometimes she gets angry. She yells at me for always being late.

Ken Ichigawa, Japan

I love to spend time with Daisuke because he makes me laugh so much. He's very funny. We share the same sense of humor, and know how to make each other cry with laughter. We enjoy talking about the funny things we did when we were children, and tell the same stupid jokes over and over again.

Word Work

6 Circle the correct word chunk.

a. Fanny and Alan have a good relationship because they always **take over each other** / **take care of each other** when they are sick.

b. Alan's girlfriend **gets angry** / **has angry** when he is late.

c. Ken prefers to **do time** / **spend time** with his friends than study.

d. Ken and Daisuke enjoy telling the same jokes and stories **over and under again** / **over and over again**.

e. Most people share a **sense of humor** / **feeling of humor** with their best friends.

Before Reading

1 Decide how to scan a text. Choose the statements you think are correct.
   a. Only look for the information you need.
   b. Look for people's names and place names.
   c. Read the first and last sentence of each paragraph.
   d. Read the text slowly and carefully.
   e. Look for dates and numbers.
   f. Look for key words.

2 What do you think "man's best friend" is? Choose one answer.
   a. technology   b. wife/girlfriend   c. dog   d. sports

3 Scan the text to check your hypothesis. Underline the words that support your answer.

While Reading

4 As you read the text, decide which of these statements you agree with.
Hollywood celebrities:
   a. have too much money.   b. are strange.
   c. are very generous.   d. know how to be happy.
   e. spend too much on their pets.

After Reading

5 Ask a partner these questions about the text.
   a. Do you think Hollywood celebrities spend too much time and money on their pets?
   b. Do you agree with Alicia Silverstone's views on people and animals?

6 What is the main idea in each paragraph? Choose one statement for each paragraph.
Paragraph 1:
   a. Celebrities make friends easily.
   b. Celebrities pay a lot of attention to their dogs.
Paragraph 2:
   a. Celebrities buy clothes for their dogs.
   b. These celebrities treat their dogs like friends.
Paragraph 3:
   a. Some celebrities take their dogs to expensive hotels for pets.
   b. Mexico is a popular place for celebrities to take a vacation.
Paragraph 4:
   a. Alicia Silverstone thinks that it is easier to like dogs than people.
   b. Alicia Silverstone thinks that animals are like people.

CD 1:
Track 8

Man's Best Friend?

[1] Many people think that it is easy for celebrities to make friends. If that is so, then why are so many famous American stars spending so much time and money on dogs? Is the saying, "Dogs are a man's best friend." true?

[2] More and more famous people are now seen with their four-legged friends. Jessica Simpson carries her dog, Daisy, around in a designer Louis Vuitton carrier. Paris Hilton dresses her Chihuahua, Tinkerbell, in different designer clothes. According to some magazines, Britney Spears spent $180 on a steak for her small Chihuahua. Even Oprah Winfrey does not like traveling without her dogs and can get upset if a hotel refuses her dogs a room!

[3] When Hollywood stars travel without their dogs, they can leave their "friends" in luxury hotels for dogs. One popular place advertises playgrounds and a pool for their dog guests. If celebrities are traveling from the USA to Los Cabos, Mexico, they can take their pet with them to the Las Ventanas al Paraiso hotel. Dogs and cats can get a massage at the pet spa before eating a special dinner. Rooms can cost up to $6,000 a night though.

[4] What explains celebrities' close relationships with their pets? As pet lover and animal activist Alicia Silverstone explained it, "Humans are greedy and selfish, and spend a lot of time taking and not giving. Animals aren't like that."

Word Work

7 **Complete the word chunks.**

a. Many people think that it is easy for celebrities to **make** _____ .

b. Why are so many famous American stars **spending so much** _____ **and** _____ on dogs?

c. _____ **and** _____ famous people are seen with their **four-legged** _____ .

d. Even Oprah Winfrey doesn't like traveling without her dogs and can **get** _____ if a hotel refuses her dogs a room!

e. As **pet** _____ **and animal** _____ Alicia Silverstone explained it, ...

My Best Friend Dan

Before Reading

1 Take two minutes to scan the text to answer these questions.

a. Where does the story take place? _____

b. How long have the writer and Dan been friends? _____

c. What does Dan have to do at the end of the story? _____

While Reading

2 As you read the story, number the pictures in order from 1 to 4.

A _____ B _____ C _____ D. _____

After Reading

3 Ask a partner these questions about the text.

Did the story:

a. make you feel sad/happy/ ...?

b. have a surprise ending/an unexpected ending/ ...?

c. have a negative ending/positive ending ...?

4 Choose the correct ending to complete the statements.

a. At the beginning of the story, Dan •   • **i.** best friends.

b. The writer helped Dan •   • **ii.** thanked the writer for being his friend.

c. The writer and Dan lived •   • **iii.** because he felt sorry for him.

d. The writer and Dan became •   • **iv.** didn't know the writer.

e. During high school, Dan •   • **v.** near each other.

f. In his speech, Dan •   • **vi.** became popular.

CD 1: Track 9

My Best Friend Dan

Walking home from school one day, I saw Dan, a kid from my school, on the other side of the road. I said to myself, "He must be a real nerd." as he was carrying a lot of books. As I continued walking, I [5] saw a group of kids run into Dan, knocking his books out of his arms and pushing him so he fell over. So, I ran over to help him, and as we were picking up his books, I saw tears in his eyes.

As I helped him stand up, I said, "Those kids [10] are stupid." He looked at me and said, "Thanks." There was a grateful smile on his face.

We started talking and soon realized that we lived near each other. We talked all the way home. Dan turned out to be a pretty cool kid. [15] We hung out all weekend and the more I got to know Dan, the more I liked him. Dan and I became best friends.

Over the next four years, he became more popular and all the girls loved him. In our senior year, Dan [20] got the best grades in our class, and had to give a speech for graduation.

As Dan started his speech, he looked at me. "Graduation is a time to thank the people who [25] helped you survive those tough years—your parents, your teachers, but mostly your friends. Being a friend is the best gift you can give. I'm going to tell you a story." I just looked at Dan in amazement as he told the story of the first [30] day we met. He had planned to drop out of school and run away from home that weekend. Dan talked of how he had emptied his locker so his mom wouldn't have to do it later and was carrying all of his books home. He looked hard [35] at me and gave me a little smile. "Thankfully, I was saved. My friend saved me from making a huge mistake." Everyone looked at Dan in shock as he told us about his weakest moment.

Word Work

5 | Complete the sentences with a word chunk from the text.

> run away from home   dropped out of school   hung out   all the way

a. My friend Sarah never studied and wasn't interested in going to college. She _____ at 16 and got a job in a fast food restaurant. She now wishes she had stayed in school.

b. I couldn't afford to fly to California for a job interview, so I drove _____ from New York. It took five days to get there.

c. Many teenagers find their lives very stressful and sometimes want to _____ .

d. I had a great time this weekend. I _____ with my best friend the whole time.

Reflection

▶ Which was your favorite text in this unit? Why?

▶ Which reading strategies did you use in this unit?

▶ Which new word chunks will you make an effort to use in the next five days? Choose at least five.

Review Reading Strategies

- Unit 1: Making hypotheses
- Unit 2: Skimming
- Unit 3: Scanning

1 Which reading strategies do these sentences describe? Read each statement and check [✓] the best answer.

	Making Hypotheses	Skimming	Scanning
a. Read the title and guess what the text is about.			
b. Read the first paragraph and the last paragraph.			
c. Only look for information you need.			
d. Look at the picture(s) and guess what the text is about.			
e. Read the first paragraph and decide if your guess was correct.			
f. Look at the whole text quickly.			
g. Look for dates and numbers.			
h. Read the first sentence of each paragraph.			
i. Look for people's names and place names.			
j. Read the last sentence of each paragraph.			
k. Look for key words (important words that tell you what the text is about).			

2 Look at the photos and the title of the article on the opposite page, and make hypotheses. What do you think the article is about? Check [✓] one or more answers.

The article will describe Jennifer Lopez's:

a. _____ childhood   **b.** _____ jewelry   **c.** _____ life

d. _____ career   **e.** _____ clothes

3 Skim the text to check your hypotheses.

4 Scan the text for names, dates, and places. Answer these questions.

a. When was Jennifer Lopez born? _____

b. Where was Jennifer Lopez born? _____

c. When did Jennifer Lopez make her first movies? _____

d. When did she marry Marc Anthony? _____

Reading

CD 1:
Track 10

Jennifer Lopez

[1] Jennifer Lynn Lopez (also known as J.Lo) is a well-known Puerto Rican-American actress and singer. Born July 24, 1970 she was raised in the Bronx area of New York City. Lopez speaks English and Spanish, and has two sisters, Leslie (a music teacher) and Lynda (a TV news presenter).

[2] Before becoming a famous celebrity, Lopez began her career as a backup dancer. She later took up acting, saying that she always wanted to do this.

[3] She started her acting career early in the 1990s with movies like *Mi Familia* and *Money Train*, but she became famous with the movie *Selena*. She followed this with *Out Of Sight*, a movie that also starred George Clooney. Since then she has appeared in many movies, including *The Wedding Planner*, *Enough*, *Maid in Manhattan*, *Shall We Dance*, and *Monster-In-Law*.

[4] J.Lo's music, mainly pop, includes the albums *J.Lo* and *On The 6*, a reference to the subway line she used to take growing up in the Bronx. In the fall of 2002, Lopez released *This Is Me ... Then*, an album which included three hugely popular singles: *Jenny From The Block*, *All I Have* (one of 2003's most popular songs), and *I'm Glad*. On November 18, 2003, she released her fifth album, *Reel Me*.

[5] On June 5, 2004, Lopez married singer Marc Anthony, who is also a Puerto Rican from New York.

[6] Since being married, the couple has often sung together, and in 2006 they acted together in the movie *El Cantante*.

[7] This was not Lopez's first marriage, actually it is her third and Anthony's second.

[8] Lopez's first marriage, which was with Ojani Onoa, ended in divorce in 1998 after just 21 months, and her second marriage, which was with Chris Judd, her former backup dancer, only lasted from 2001 to 2002. Between her first two marriages, Lopez dated the singer and designer Puff Daddy, breaking up after a shooting incident in a New York nightclub. She then dated and was engaged to the actor Ben Affleck, but their marriage, planned for September 13, 2003, was called off a few days before the wedding. In January 2004 the couple split.

Comprehension Check

1 Decide if the statements are true (T) or false (F), according to the article.

a.   T   F   Jennifer Lopez was born in Puerto Rico.

b.   T   F   Jennifer Lopez was an actor before she took up singing.

c.   T   F   Jennifer Lopez has been married three times.

d.   T   F   Jennifer Lopez married Ben Affleck on September 13, 2003.

2 The word "this" at the end of the second paragraph refers to:

a. singing   b. dancing   c. acting   d. becoming famous

3 According to the article, Jennifer Lopez:

a. always wanted to act with George Clooney.

b. decided to be an actor in the early 1990s.

c. wanted to be an actor for a long time.

d. didn't appear in a lot of movies in the 1990s.

4 The word "incident" in the final paragraph is closest in meaning to:

a. accident   b. fight   c. festival   d. practice

5 According to the text, which statement about Jennifer Lopez is NOT true?

a. Jennifer Lopez and her first husband divorced after less than two years of marriage.

b. Jennifer Lopez's second husband was one of her backup dancers.

c. Jennifer Lopez was engaged to Puff Daddy and Ben Affleck before she married Marc Anthony.

d. Both Marc Anthony and Jennifer Lopez have been married before.

More Word Chunks

1 Complete the sentences, using these word chunks from Units 1, 2 and 3.

over again	result	interests	humor	common
go on	addition	time	routine	business

a. My best friend is very funny. He has a good **sense of** _____ and makes me laugh a lot.

b. I run five miles every morning. It is a very important part of my **daily** _____ .

c. This summer I want to _____ **vacation** to Kyoto in Japan.

d. My friend has his own Internet company. He **runs the** _____ from home.

e. I am very busy during the week, but on the weekend I like to **spend** _____ **with** my friends and family.

f. I hate that song. I heard it **over and** _____ on the radio this summer.

g. **In** _____ **to** dancing, singing, and acting, Jennifer Lopez also designs clothes.

h. Jennifer Lopez and Marc Anthony **share the same** _____ **in** singing and acting.

i. Often married couples who **have nothing in** _____ end up getting divorced.

j. Jennifer Lopez is probably adventurous and creative **as a** _____ **of** being the second child.

2 | **In Unit 1 we learned about the word chunks "interested in each other" and "living with each other."**

Sue and Jim were neighbors for five years, but they were never interested in each other.
Sue and Jim are now married and living with each other.

Here are some other word chunks with "each other."

hang out with each other	known each other	take care of each other
talk to each other	met each other	learn from each other

Complete the sentences with a word chunk from the box.

a. Chris Judd and Jennifer Lopez _____ on a concert tour because he was her backup dancer.

b. Marc Anthony and Jennifer Lopez have _____ for a long time. They met before she separated from Ben Affleck.

c. Because they are both singers, Lopez and Anthony are able to _____ and help each other become better singers.

d. When they are feeling sad or upset, most married couples _____ about their problems. This often helps them feel better.

e. Couples who have a good marriage _____ when they are sick and as they grow old.

f. Famous singers and actors like to _____ because they enjoy each other's company. They share similar interests and problems, and they can also help each other's careers.

Warm Up

1 With a partner, guess what difficult decision these friends are making.

2 Read the text. Do you think the friends made the right decision?

After eating dinner at a restaurant, Sunni and her friends got the bill and noticed that the server forgot to charge them for drinks and dessert. They decided not to say anything. The dinner was expensive and it was the server's mistake.

Reading Strategy: Making predictions

Good readers make predictions while they are reading. They think about what action, topic, or words will come next.

For example, "I was on vacation in Hong Kong, and I couldn't believe it when I saw ..." Tell a partner how you think this sentence will end.

Did you predict the sentence ends with "Jackie Chan," or "my friend from school"? If you thought that the sentence ends with someone famous or someone the writer knows, you would be making a good prediction. Making and checking predictions while you are reading will help you understand and stay interested in the text.

Strategy in Focus

1 Tell a partner what you think is happening in the picture.

2 Now read the text. With a partner, predict what the writer says to his girlfriend.

It was my birthday last week and my girlfriend gave me a sweater. It was not my taste at all. She asked me if I liked it, and I said, ...

a. "Why didn't you give me money?"

b. "Not really. Can we take it back to the store tomorrow?"

c. "Of course I do. It's great."

3 Tell a partner what you think is happening in the picture.

4 Now read the text. With a partner, predict what the writer tells Chiya.

My friend Chiya spent all night working on an English paper and didn't have time to do her math homework. She asked me if it was OK to copy my homework. I told her ...

Feedback:

Activity 2. The correct prediction is probably c. Many people think it is polite to thank someone for a gift even if they don't like it. You can use your own experience of giving and receiving gifts to make this prediction.

Activity 4. Possible predictions are:

- she should do the homework by herself. She will not learn by copying.
- just this time. But never again. I don't want to get caught.
- to ask another friend. I don't think it is right to copy.

It is important that you make predictions when you read. It is also important to understand if your prediction was correct. Making predictions helps you enjoy and focus on the text.

Dear Hannah's Advice Column

Before Reading

1 **Look at the title of the text and the photo. What kind of text is it?**

a. News article.
c. A letter asking for advice.
b. An advertisement.
d. A complaint letter.

2 **Read the beginning of Sang-mi's letter below. Then predict Sang-mi's problem with Lisa.**

Dear Hannah:
I am 16 years old and a high school student. I enjoy school, get good grades, and have a close group of friends. My problem is with my best friend, Lisa. We are in all the same classes and we used to always help each other study. Recently, however, she is very ...

a. competitive with me.
b. rude to me.
c. angry with me.

3 **Read the next part of the letter below. Then predict what Sang-mi writes next.**

Lisa always wants to compare our grades, and gets upset if my grades are better. Next week, we have an English exam and ...

a. it will be difficult.
b. I don't like English.
c. she doesn't want to study with me.

4 **Predict what Sang-mi will do at the end of the letter.**

a. Describe a plan to change Lisa.
c. Ask for advice.
b. Invite Hannah to visit their school.

While Reading

5 **Read Sang-mi's letter and check your predictions.**

6 **Predict what Hannah will advise Sang-mi to do.**

a. Sang-mi should ignore the problem.
c. Sang-mi should find new friends.
b. Sang-mi should tell Lisa how she feels.

7 **Read Hannah's reply and check your prediction.**

After Reading

8 **Ask a partner these questions about the text.**

a. Do you agree with Hannah's advice?
b. What would you do in Sang-mi's situation?

CD 1:
Track 11

Dear Hannah's Advice Column

Dear Hannah,

I am 16 years old and a high school student. I enjoy school, get good grades, and have a close group of friends. My problem is with my best
[5] friend, Lisa. We are in all the same classes and we used to always help each other study. Recently, however, she is very competitive with me. Lisa always wants to compare our grades, and gets upset if my grades are better. Next
[10] week, we have an English exam and she doesn't want to study with me.

She has become so competitive, and I don't know what to do. I don't want to lose our friendship, but at the same time I don't want to
[15] compete with her anymore. What should I do?

Yours,

Sang-mi

Dear Sang-mi,

You can talk with her and explain that you really enjoy her friendship but you are uncomfortable when she compares grades. Continue to do the
[20] best you can with your own grades and studies. Let Lisa enjoy her good grades, and you should enjoy yours too. Hopefully, Lisa will respect your friendship and you'll feel more comfortable.

[25] Yours,

Hannah

Dear Hannah,

In one month, I am moving with my family to a new city ...

Word Work

9 Circle the word chunks that are true for the text.

Sang-mi is a **high school student** / **college student** and enjoys school. She gets **low scores** / **good grades** and has a close group of friends. However, she has one friend, Lisa, who is now very competitive. They used to **help each other** / **help others**, but not anymore. Now, Lisa wants to get higher grades than Sang-mi and **gets upset** / **gets tired** if she doesn't. Sang-mi doesn't want them to **lose their cool** / **lose their friendship** but she is **having trouble** / **having fun** staying friends with Lisa.

Before Reading

1 **What could help you choose a career? Choose one or more answers.**

a. Think about what you enjoy doing.
b. Do an internship at a company.
c. Listen to music to relax you.
d. Read about different careers.
e. Think about what's important to you in life.
f. Talk to people about their jobs.

2 **You will read these sentences in the text. Predict which ending matches the beginning of each sentence.**

a. If you follow these three steps, •

b. Before you decide upon a career, •

c. Also, talk to people already doing jobs that you find interesting, •

d. Most people change jobs several times during their work life, •

• i. think about your interests, and your talents and values, and then think about jobs that fit them.

• ii. so don't put too much pressure on yourself to make the perfect decision.

• iii. you'll have a good chance of finding a career that will keep you interested for a long time.

• iv. and try out careers by taking internships or part-time jobs.

While Reading

3 **As you read the text, check your predictions.**

After Reading

4 **Ask a partner these questions about the text.**

a. Do you agree with the author's advice on how to choose a career?
b. What else would you recommend?

5 **According to the article, when should you ask these questions? Write the number for each step.**

a. What kind of qualifications do I require to get this job? _____
b. What do I enjoy doing? _____
c. Is money more important to me than time off? _____
d. What do I do well? _____
e. Do I like working with people or working by myself? _____
f. How much does this job pay? _____

**CD 1:
Track 12**

Choosing the Right Career

For many students, choosing a career is the most important life decision they must make at school. But, choosing the right career is not easy. So how do you find one that you will enjoy [5] and find satisfying?

If you follow these three steps, you will have a good chance of finding a career that will keep you interested for a long time.

Step One: Reflection

[10] Before you decide upon a career, think about your interests and your talents, and then think about jobs that fit them. Ask yourself: What do I enjoy doing? What do I do well? Then think about the jobs that match these interests and talents.

[15] Step Two: Planning

Next, learn about your career options. See if the library has books describing different kinds of work, the typical qualifications required, and the typical salaries for various jobs. Also, talk [20] to people already doing jobs that you find interesting, and try out careers by taking internships or part-time jobs.

Step Three: Selection

After you have spent time on steps one and [25] two, consider what kind of personality you have and what your values are: what is important to you. Perhaps you like working face to face with people. If so, a job as a computer programmer may not be the best option. If you like the [30] security of getting a monthly salary, then starting your own business probably is not for you.

Finally, remember that you can always change your mind. Most people change jobs several times during their working life, so do not put too [35] much pressure on yourself to make the perfect decision right now. Your first job right after college probably will not be your career thirty years from now. Be flexible and allow yourself to change if you are not satisfied with your [40] chosen career.

Word Work

6 Complete the sentences using the word chunks below.

be flexible	changed her mind	put too much pressure on
several times	right after	

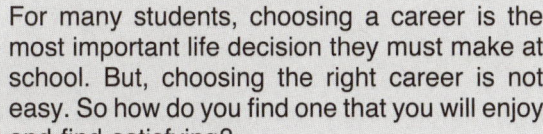

a. After changing jobs _____, I eventually found a job that I really liked.

b. I was lucky: I found a job _____ leaving school.

c. Parents and teachers tend to _____ youngsters to pass the university entrance exam and get a good job.

d. You should _____ and change your job if you are unhappy at work.

e. Sarah wanted to be a doctor, but she _____. Now she wants to go to graduate school to study law.

Before Reading

1 *The Magic Fish* is a fable (a story with a moral lesson). Look at the words and sentences below. With a partner, decide what will happen in the fable.

fisherman	old shack	wife	The fisherman didn't know what to do.
magical fish	wish	a castle	She started to complain.

While Reading

2 The pictures below illustrate this popular fable. After each paragraph, stop, and predict which picture will come next.

A _____

B _____

C _____

D _____

E _____

F _____

After Reading

3 What do you think the moral of this story is?

a. You shouldn't trust people.

b. You should trust your own judgment.

c. Husbands should listen to their wives.

4 Think of three wishes that you would make if you met a magic fish. Are the wishes for yourself, for someone you know, or for others in the world?

The Magic Fish

A fisherman lived with his wife in an old shack by the sea. Each day he caught a fish, and cooked it for his wife. One day he caught a talking fish. The fish asked the fisherman to let
[5] him live, and the fisherman agreed. For the rest of the day, he caught nothing else.

When the fisherman got home empty-handed, his wife asked what happened. He told her about the magical fish. "What did you get in return?" his
[10] wife asked. "Nothing," said the fisherman, which made his wife very angry. "It's a magical fish so ask it to grant your wish. I hate my shack. Ask the fish for a nice house," she demanded. The man didn't want to trouble the fish but he didn't
[15] want his wife to get angry either. He did not know if he should listen to his heart or his wife.

The next day the fisherman went to the sea and told the fish about his wife's wish. When he got home, his wife was standing in front of a beautiful house.

[20] For a week, she was happy but then she started to complain. "Go back and ask for a castle," she said. "If you don't, I'll be unhappy forever." The fisherman didn't want a bigger house but he didn't want his wife to be unhappy. Again, he did not
[25] know if he should listen to his heart or his wife.

However, the next day, he returned to the sea and spoke to the fish again. When he got home, his wife was standing in front of a large castle.

Life was good for a few days but early one
[30] morning, the fisherman's wife said, "I want to be queen of the land." The fisherman couldn't believe it. "I won't go," he told her. "Then, I will never speak to you again," she said.

After a troubled night's sleep, the fisherman
[35] went back to the fish and in a nervous voice told him the latest wish. The fish told the man to return to his wife and said she would be queen of her land.

When he got home, his wife was crying and
[40] standing in front of their old shack.

Word Work

5 Complete the paragraph with word chunks from the story.

home	one	couldn't	day	standing	what

I buy a lottery ticket every week. _____ **day** last summer I bought my usual lottery ticket number. The **next** _____ I was reading the paper and I saw my lottery ticket number. I _____ **believe it**. I won the lottery. When I **got** _____, my wife was _____ **in front of the house** talking to our neighbor. I **didn't know** _____ **to do**. Should I tell her now or wait until next week for her birthday.

Reflection

▶ Which was your favorite text in this unit? Why?

▶ Which reading strategies did you use in this unit?

▶ Which new word chunks will you make an effort to use in the next five days? Choose at least five.

Warm Up

1 With a partner, take turns describing the pictures.

A _____

B _____

2 Take one minute to skim the blog entries on the next page. Then write the name of the writer under the correct picture in activity 1.

Reading Strategy: Making inferences

To **make an inference**, you read a text, sentence, or phrase, think about it, and understand things about the text that are not mentioned.

For example, after reading, "Suzy is relaxing on her sofa." you can infer:

- Suzy is a woman; Suzy is a woman's name and the writer uses "her" to refer to Suzy.
- Suzy is probably at home; we usually find sofas in homes and we know that it is Suzy's sofa.
- Suzy is probably lying down on her sofa; many people lie down when relaxing on their sofa.

The writer doesn't tell us that Suzy is a woman who is lying on her sofa at home, but we can make these inferences from the information in the text.

When you read effectively, you make inferences to help you understand the text and the author better.

Strategy in Focus

Read Vanessa and Min-ho's blog entries. Check [✓] the inferences you can make.

a. _____ Vanessa's parents are rich.

b. _____ When Vanessa was young, she was often sick.

c. _____ Vanessa thinks reading improved her grades.

d. _____ Min-ho is hard working.

e. _____ Min-ho always wanted to be a travel agent.

f. _____ Going to China was a positive experience for Min-ho.

I was a quiet student at high school and spent most of my time studying. I needed to get good grades and get into a good college. After college, I realized I had no idea what I wanted to do next and I didn't have any real friends. I worked in a restaurant for the summer and saved enough money to go to China for two months. I came back changed. While traveling, I had learned some Chinese and made friends from all over the world as well as China. Some of them are coming to visit me next summer.

Min-ho Lee, Pusan, South Korea

When I was seven years old, I caught the flu and stayed home from school. My parents had to work, so my neighbor came over to look after me. She read to me for hours and it felt like I was listening to a movie. She started my interest in reading. I was never a good student, but my grades started improving at school. When I graduate next spring, I have a job teaching English to high school students.

Vanessa Perez, San Francisco, the United States

Feedback:
The correct answers are c. d. and f.

c. We can infer that Vanessa thinks reading improved her grades because she says before she was interested in reading she wasn't a good student. Now that she is interested in reading, her grades are better.

d. We can infer Min-ho is hard-working because he says he spent most of his time studying in high school and he worked during his summer holiday in a restaurant to save money to travel. A lot of students like to hang out with friends at high school and ask their parents for money to travel. Min-ho preferred to work instead.

f. We can infer that Min-ho had a positive experience because he says he changed and now has friends that will visit him in Korea and he speaks some Chinese. Most people would agree that having friends and learning something new are positive things.

Before Reading

1 What do you think the phrase "a college dropout" means? Choose one answer. Scan the text to check your hypothesis.

a. A student who graduates from college at a very young age.

b. A student who leaves college without graduating.

c. A student who changes his/her major after one year of college.

While Reading

2 As you read the text, decide which experiences were life-changing for Steve Jobs. Check [✓] three statements.

a. _____ Jobs made a speech at Stanford University.

b. _____ At 17, Jobs went to college.

c. _____ Jobs read a quotation about how to live life.

d. _____ Jobs was fired from Apple Computers.

After Reading

3 Ask a partner this question about the text.

Which experience do you think changed Steve Jobs' life the most?

4 Read each statement and check [✓] the inference you can make.

a. Jobs' biological mother was a college student who felt unable to cope as a young mother so put him up for adoption.

   i. _____ Jobs' biological mother was not married.

   ii. _____ Jobs' biological mother didn't graduate from college.

b. Jobs' adopted parents were simple working-class people.

   i. _____ Jobs' adopted parents didn't work.

   ii. _____ Jobs' adopted parents weren't rich.

c. After six months of college, Jobs decided it was not for him.

   i. _____ Jobs didn't think college was useful for him.

   ii. _____ Jobs spent six months at college.

5 Check [✓] the inferences you can make about the text.

a. _____ Jobs likes to take risks.

b. _____ Jobs has many creative ideas.

c. _____ Jobs doesn't like to work.

d. _____ Jobs is only interested in making money.

e. _____ Jobs has children.

f. _____ Getting fired from Apple helped Jobs' career.

6 Underline the words, phrases, or sentences that support your inferences in activity 5.

CD 1:
Track 14

The College Dropout

Steve Jobs is famous for starting Apple Computers. In a speech to graduating students at Stanford University, Jobs told students about some of his life-changing experiences. Jobs believes these [5] experiences helped him achieve success.

Jobs' biological mother was a college student who felt unable to cope as a young mother so put him up for adoption. Jobs' adopted parents were simple working-class people. When Jobs [10] was 17, his parents used their savings to send him to college.

After six months of college, Jobs decided it was not for him. Around that time, he had read a quotation that went something like, "If you live [15] each day as if it was your last, someday you'll most certainly be right." The quotation made him think about his life and his future. He started to question if he should stay in college. Was he doing what he really wanted to do? Eventually, [20] he decided he had to change something; he decided to drop out of college.

Jobs was lucky because he knew what he loved to do. He started Apple Computers in his parents' garage with a friend when he was 20. In just [25] ten years, Apple grew into a $2 billion company. However in 1985, Jobs was fired from the company.

Jobs was shocked. In an instant, he lost everything. Jobs quickly realized that he still loved what he [30] did, and over the next five years, he started two highly successful companies, NeXT and Pixar. Jobs also met his future wife, Laurene.

Jobs is now happily married with a family, working for Apple again and living every day as [35] if it were his last.

Word Work

7 Complete the paragraph about rap and hip-hop musician Kanye West with word chunks from the text.

achieved	drop out	all over	lost

Kanye was a student at Chicago State University, but decided **to** _____ **of college** to work on his music career. He had a serious car crash in 2002 that left him in hospital. He nearly _____ **everything**, but the experience taught him the meaning of life. In 2004 Kanye _____ **success** with his first album The College Dropout. Over five million copies of the album have been sold _____ **the world**.

8 Choose word chunks from the text and write three sentences about yourself.

a. _____

b. _____

c. _____

Take a Life-Changing Vacation

Before Reading

1 Take one minute to skim the advertisement. What is the main idea of the advertisement?

a. Going on vacation to see new places.
b. Going on vacation to relax and have fun.
c. Going on vacation to work and help the local people.

2 Scan the text to match the volunteer project with the correct country.

improve school rooms   paint homes   work with pre-school children
teach school subjects   practice English   plant trees

Country	Volunteer Projects
Senegal	_____
Australia	_____
Guatemala	_____
Belize	_____
United States	_____
China	_____

While Reading

3 As you read the text, decide if you would like to go on a volunteer vacation.

After Reading

4 Ask a partner these questions about the text.
a. Would you like to go on a volunteer vacation?
b. Which country would you like to go to?

5 Check [✓] the inferences that you can make about the advertisement.

a. _____ Grace Chan had a positive experience in Senegal.
b. _____ Grace Chan had a negative experience in Senegal.
c. _____ Vacation volunteers help communities and people who don't have much money.
d. _____ Vacation volunteers only help communities and people who live in rural areas.
e. _____ There are a lot of damaged buildings in Jamaica.
f. _____ Jamaica needs to build more hotels for tourism.

6 Underline the words, phrases, or sentences in the text that support your inferences in activity 5.

Take a Life-Changing Vacation

You can make a difference to the life of others by signing up for a volunteer vacation.

"I learned more about myself during the three months volunteering in Senegal than I have my [5] whole life."—Grace Chan, Vancouver

Volunteer Opportunities:

Australia: Work on community or agricultural projects, such as home repair and painting, building construction, or planting trees.

[10] **Guatemala:** Work with disadvantaged preschool children and their families.

Belize: Help with community development projects, such as improving school classrooms, or expanding community center buildings.

[15] **Senegal:** Teach school subjects, help in a hospital, or work on simple construction projects.

The United States: Work in Florida or Mississippi on community projects, including painting and repairing local homes, cleaning up town or state [20] parks, and teaching disadvantaged children.

China: Volunteers with a medical or legal background can choose to spend their time working with students at medical centers or law schools. Others can spend their time practicing English [25] conversation with local students and teachers.

Global Volunteers History:

After running a successful computer business for several years, husband and wife Ray and Carla Hill decided they both wanted a career change and to [30] do something different. They decided to take a six-month vacation, working on a community project in Australia. This trip inspired them to start World [35] Volunteering, which has sent about 2,000 volunteers on projects around the world since 1995. As Carla says, "If we reach out and [40] help others in need, we can change the face of the planet."

Word Work

7 Match the words to make word chunks from the text. Then choose a word chunk and write a sentence about yourself.

a. make •	•	**i** about myself
b. learn •	•	**ii** whole life
c. spend •	•	**iii** a difference
d. do •	•	**iv** something different
e. my •	•	**v** their time

Before Reading

1 Look at the title of the text and pictures. Decide what you think the story is about.

a. A teenager who didn't want to go to college.

b. A teenager who wanted a part-time job in a factory.

c. A father who forced his daughter to work in a factory.

While Reading

2 As you read the story, order the pictures from 1 to 4.

A _____

B _____

C _____

D _____

After Reading

3 What inferences can you make? Write "Yes," "No" or "Maybe."

a. The writer has a good relationship with her father. _____

b. The writer thinks her father is strict. _____

c. The writer had a good imagination. _____

d. The people in the factory looked happy. _____

e. Working in the factory looked fun. _____

f. The factory building was ugly. _____

g. The writer studied hard at school and college after the factory visit. _____

h. The writer is grateful to her father. _____

i. The writer is an interpreter for the UN. _____

j. The writer is happily married. _____

4 Underline the words in the text that support your inferences in activity 3.

CD 1: Track 16

The Brick Factory

When I was a teenager growing up in Russia, I wanted to leave school and have my own life. The only way I could do this was to work in the local brick factory in my town, or get married. I was very
[5] nervous when I told my father I wanted to leave school. I thought he would say, "No! You are going to college." He took me by surprise when he said, "OK. Let's go to the brick factory."

Two days later, he took me to the factory. I
[10] had a very romantic idea of working in a factory. I had imagined everyone to be friends working together and having fun. I even imagined there would be music and singing. I guess I had watched too many movies as a teenager.

[15] When we arrived at the factory gates, my father spoke to the guard and one minute later we were inside. My father said, "Take your time. Look around." I walked around the factory looking at the building, the workers, and listening to the
[20] noise. It was horrible. I ran back to my father and said, "I want to go home."

He asked me, "What do you think of the factory?"

"It's terrible," I replied.

"And marriage is even worse!" he said.

I went back to school the next day thinking
[25] about studying hard so I could get into a good college. I enjoyed studying English so I decided to major in languages at college. Thanks to my father and our trip to the brick factory, I now work at the United Nations and my father is very
[30] proud of me. I married a very good man and my life is much better than it would have been working in the factory!

Word Work

5 Correct the mistakes in these word chunks, without looking at the text.

a. When I was a teenager, I wanted to **end school** and have my own life. _____

b. He **had me by surprise** when he said, "OK. Let's go to the brick factory." _____

c. "And marriage is **very worse**!" he said. _____

d. I now work at the United Nations and my father is **very proud at me**. _____

e. My life is **much better that** it would have been working in the factory! _____

Reflection

▶ Which was your favorite text in this unit? Why?

▶ Which reading strategies did you use in this unit?

▶ Which new word chunks will you make an effort to use in the next five days? Choose at least five.

6 Unexpected Events

Warm Up

1 Look at the two pictures and predict what will happen next. Tell a partner.
   a. The man gives the woman a reward.
   b. The woman keeps the wallet for herself.

2 Now read the text and check your prediction.
The woman hands the wallet back to the man and receives $20 as a reward. Unfortunately, she drops her reward on her way back home.

Reading Strategy: Interpreting

To read effectively, you often need to **interpret** the text. Ask yourself, "What is the writer saying?" Consider this example:

What does the customer mean by, "You must be joking"? Does she think the waiter is joking? No. You can interpret the customer to mean the bill is very expensive and he wasn't expecting such a large bill.

Interpreting the text is an important part of reading. If you make **interpretations** about the text, you will understand it more fully.

$160! You must be joking.

Strategy in Focus

1 **Read the passage. While reading, decide what the phrase in bold means.**

a. She won't be able to remember him.
b. She will stop hoping to be his girlfriend.
c. She will forget his name.

Subway Coincidence

Once I was in love with someone who already had a girlfriend. The situation was making me ill so one day, when I was with my friends, I told them, "**I should forget about him.**" I decided that if I ever saw him with his girlfriend, I would do my best to forget about him. Five minutes later we were waiting for a subway train. As we were waiting, the train going in the other direction stopped, and directly in front of me I could see them together on the train holding hands.

Feedback:

The correct answer is b. Men and women often say "I should forget about her/him." when they know the person they love does not love them.

2 **Read the passage. While reading, decide what the sentence in bold means.**

a. The writer was too young to realize the meeting was a big coincidence.
b. The writer was surprised to see Dominic in Egypt.

Chance Meeting

When I was young, my family lived in Thailand because of my father's work. I met and became friends with children from all over the world. One of my friends in Thailand was a boy called Dominic. When I was five, my family returned to England. I said goodbye to all my friends and hoped that we would be able to play together again one day. My parents decided to take a vacation in Egypt on the way back to England. My father and I were walking around the pyramids when, from around a corner, Dominic and his father appeared. **Because we were only five at the time, neither Dominic nor I found this even slightly odd.** Our dads, of course, were very surprised.

Feedback:

The correct answer is a.   The writer is saying that five-year-olds don't understand the great distance between Thailand and Egypt, they didn't realize that seeing each other was a really big coincidence.

Lost and Found

Before Reading

1 Take one minute to scan the news story and answer the questions.

a. What was lost? _____

b. Who lost it? _____

c. Who found it? _____

While Reading

2 As you read the news story, decide if you agree [✓] or disagree [✗] with the interpretations of these sentences.

	Interpretation	✓ / ✗
a. "Kim looked through the garbage and all the buildings where she worked but came up empty-handed." (line 6)	After looking everywhere, Kim could not find her wallet.	☐
b. "She went home heartbroken, believing that she had lost her money for good." (line 8)	She thought it was good that her money was missing.	☐
c. "'I couldn't believe it when they called me,' she said." (line 24)	She was surprised by the news.	☐
d. "He has a very big heart." (line 25)	He was born with a large heart.	☐
e. "If someone else had found it, the money would be gone." (line 25)	Most people wouldn't give the money back.	☐

After Reading

3 Ask a partner these questions about the homeless man.

a. Do you think the homeless man did the right thing?

b. What would you have done if you were the homeless man?

4 Check [✓] the inferences you can make about the news story. Underline the parts of the text that support your inferences.

a. _____ Kim Bogue emigrated from Thailand to America.

b. _____ Kim could buy an airline ticket to Thailand for $900 or less.

c. _____ Kim couldn't go to Thailand if she didn't find her wallet and money.

d. _____ Sherry Wesley didn't trust the homeless man.

e. _____ The homeless man gave back the wallet for the $100 reward.

CD 1:
Track 17

Lost and Found

Kim Bogue, a janitor in California, worked overtime to save money for a trip to Thailand to visit her family and friends. She saved over $900 and was planning to buy a ticket, but she lost [5] her wallet with all her money and credit cards.

Kim looked through the garbage and all the buildings where she worked but came up empty-handed. She went home heartbroken, believing that she had lost her money for good.

[10] While Kim was home, sad and depressed, a homeless man was searching through the garbage looking for things to sell. As he was looking through a garbage bag, he found something wrapped in a plastic bag.

[15] The homeless man, who did not want to be identified, took the wallet to Sherry Wesley. Wesley knew the man from her volunteer work at a homeless shelter. "He came to me with the wad of money and said, 'This probably belongs to someone that you [20] work with, can you return it?'" Wesley works in one of the buildings that Bogue cleans and she knew Bogue had lost her wallet.

Bogue was amazed when she heard the good news. "I couldn't believe it when they called me," [25] she said. "He has a very big heart. If someone else had found it, the money would be gone."

As a reward, Bogue gave the man $100. The homeless man gave half of the money to Wesley, who then donated it to charity.

Word Work

5 **Change the bold words in the sentence with a word chunk from the text.**

a. I **worked extra hours** in the store, so I could save money for my summer vacation.

_____

b. She usually spends the weekend with **the people she is closest to**. _____

c. I couldn't find my cell phone last night. I **searched through** my bags and closets at home but couldn't find it. _____

d. Everyone loves my father because he **is such a generous man**. _____

Twin Expectations

Before Reading

1 **Look at the title of the news story and the photo. What do you think the text is about?**
a. Twin sisters who are both having a baby at the same time.
b. Twin sisters marrying twin brothers.
c. Two friends who are both pregnant with twins at the same time.

While Reading

2 **As you read the news story, decide what the writer is saying about the following:**
a. ". . . and now, at 35, they are both experiencing "morning sickness."" (line 3)
  i. Both women have a disease.
  ii. Both women are pregnant.

b. "However, after another three years and having spent over $25,000 on in vitro fertilization, Tasha changed her mind." (line 20)
  i. Tasha thought it was impossible for her to become pregnant.
  ii. Tasha didn't want to have a baby anymore.

c. "At 35, Raquel only had a 50 percent chance of having a baby." (line 24)
  i. It can be difficult to get pregnant at 35.
  ii. 50 percent of women get pregnant at 35.

d. "So it's kind of funny how things worked out." (line 34)
  i. Tasha and her husband laugh at the situation a lot.
  ii. It is a big coincidence that the friends became pregnant at the same time.

After Reading

3 **Decide if the statements are true (T) or false (F).**
a. T F Tasha and Raquel met for the first time at the doctor's office.
b. T F Tasha and Raquel are having twins.
c. T F Tasha spent a lot of money and many years trying to have a baby.
d. T F Tasha asked Raquel to have her baby.
e. T F Tasha paid Raquel $25,000.
f. T F Tasha and her husband are the biological parents of Raquel's twins.

Twin Expectations

Tasha Riddle and Raquel Mitola have been best friends since they were eleven. They have shared many experiences since childhood and now, at 35, they are both experiencing "morning sickness."

[5] Not only are they both pregnant, but they are both expecting twins which are due on the same day, June 7. However, there is one more thing that they have in common. The four babies have the same biological parents; Tasha and her [10] husband, John.

The Riddles had tried to have a baby for four years without success. Tasha's best friend, Raquel, wanted to help and offered to be a surrogate mother where she would have Tasha and John's [15] baby. Raquel's husband said, "It just seemed like a natural thing to do because Tasha needed help and Raquel enjoyed being pregnant."

Tasha had wanted to give birth herself so she did not accept Raquel's offer straight away. [20] However, after another three years and having spent over $25,000 on in vitro fertilization (IVF), Tasha changed her mind.

Using IVF, doctors implanted two of Tasha and John's embryos in Raquel. At 35, Raquel only [25] had a 50 percent chance of having a baby. Surprisingly, Raquel became pregnant with her friends' babies at the first attempt. Doctors had also implanted Tasha with four of her embryos and to everyone's amazement, Tasha found out [30] she was also pregnant with twins.

Although it was a shock, the Riddles are very happy that they are having four babies. Tasha said, "We always said we wanted to raise our kids together. So it's kind of funny how things worked [35] out. Now we're having my babies together."

Word Work

4 | Match the word chunk with its definition. Then choose one word chunk and write a sentence about yourself or someone you know.

a. expecting twins •   • i. would like to be a parent

b. have in common •   • ii. being pregnant with two babies

c. want to raise children •   • iii. tried once

d. to change her mind •   • iv. share an experience or characteristic

e. the first attempt •   • v. choose a different idea

A Surprise Gold Medal

Before Reading

1 Look at the photo of the sportsman Billy Mills. Read the first and last sentence of each paragraph in the text. Decide if the statements are true (T) or false (F).

a.	**T**	**F**	Billy Mills is an Irish American.
b.	**T**	**F**	He was one of the fastest runners at his university.
c.	**T**	**F**	Everyone expected Billy to win a gold medal.
d.	**T**	**F**	Billy was slower than the other runners in the race.
e.	**T**	**F**	Billy won an Olympic medal for the 100-meter sprint.

While Reading

2 As you read the text, decide what the writer is saying about the following:

a. "Childhood was not easy for Billy." (line 3)
 i. Billy did not have a happy childhood.
 ii. Billy had to study harder than other children.

b. ". . . he lost his mother when he was seven, and his father passed away ..." (line 4)
 i. Both of his parents died.
 ii. His parents divorced and they both left home.

c. "Although he was on the U.S. team, many people did not expect anything from Billy." (line 21)
 i. No one believed he could win a medal.
 ii. Everyone was surprised that Billy was a world record holder.

d. "Everyone else was out of the race ..." (line 33)
 i. The other runners had already finished the race.
 ii. The other runners were far behind.

After Reading

3 Ask a partner these questions about the text.

a. Why do you think Billy Mills was able to win the Olympic gold medal?

b. What do you think the writer means when he says, "At first he focused on military life"?

c. Why did nobody think Billy would win the Olympic 10,000-meter medal?

A Surprise Gold Medal

Billy Mills, a Native American, was born and raised on a reservation in the United States. Childhood was not easy for Billy. His family was not well off; he lost his mother when he was [5] seven, and his father passed away five years later. After his father's death, Billy was sent to a boarding school. At school Billy started running to help him forget his problems. To his amazement, he found that he had a talent for [10] running and broke a number of high school records. As a result of his running, he was given an athletic scholarship to the University of Kansas.

At the University of Kansas, Billy continued to [15] win many competitions. After graduation he joined the United States Marine Corps. At first he focused on military life, but he soon returned to running. He did well enough to race in the 1964 Tokyo Olympics in the 10,000 meters and [20] marathon events.

Although he was on the U.S. team, many people did not expect anything from Billy. In the 10,000 meters, Billy was almost a minute slower than the favorite, Ron Clarke of Australia. The other [25] favorite to win the Olympic gold was Mohammad Gammoudi of Tunisia. The rest of the runners included Olympic gold medal and world record holders. All eyes were focused on the front runners, not on Billy.

[30] When the race started, everyone was surprised to see Billy Mills at the front with Ron Clarke. For much of the race, the two ran together with Gammoudi just behind them. Everyone else was out of the race, and the crowd expected Mills to [35] tire and slow down.

Near the end of the race, Gammoudi ran between Clark and Mills and pushed them aside. The two of them almost fell over and Mills dropped behind into third place. However, Mills was [40] determined not to lose. He raced ahead to win the gold, and set an Olympic 10,000 meter record. He was the first Native American to win the Olympic 10,000-meter race.

Word Work

4 Use these word chunks to write sentences about Billy Mills, without looking at the text.

a. born and raised: _____

b. not well off: _____

c. had a talent for: _____

d. As a result of: _____

Reflection

▶ Which was your favorite text in this unit? Why?

▶ Which reading strategies did you use in this unit?

▶ Which new word chunks will you make an effort to use in the next five days? Choose at least five.

Review Reading Strategies

- Unit 4: Making predictions
- Unit 5: Making inferences
- Unit 6: Interpreting

1 Which reading strategies do these sentences describe? Read each statement and check [✓] the best answer.

	Making Predictions	Making Inferences	Interpreting
a. Understand things about the text that are not mentioned.	_____	_____	_____
b. Guess what will happen next.	_____	_____	_____
c. Think about what the writer means.	_____	_____	_____
d. Guess what the next word or phrase will be.	_____	_____	_____

2 Read the beginning of the text *Modern Social Networking* below, and predict which words come next. Choose one or more answers.

Throughout history, humans have had an urge to make social connections. Making friends is something that most people do naturally when meeting people through ...

a. Internet chatrooms   **b.** cell phones   **c.** family and friends   **d.** work or school

3 As you read the text, decide what the writer is saying about the following:

a. "Throughout history, humans have had an urge to make social connections." (paragraph 1)
   i. People have always felt the need to make friends.
   ii. In the past, people felt pressure to make friends.

b. "For many, these sites have made a positive difference in their lives by widening their social circles." (paragraph 4)
   i. Many people have made a lot of new friends because of MySpace.
   ii. Many people go to a lot of parties now because of MySpace.

c. ". . . then changing their mind . . ." (paragraph 4)
   i. They decided not to give them a job.
   ii. They weren't intelligent enough to get a job.

4 Check [✓] the inferences you can make about the text. Underline the words, phrases, or sentences that support your inferences.

a. _____ Young people tend to meet new friends on the Internet rather than through family and friends.
b. _____ Young people don't have much in common with older people.
c. _____ My Space is popular because it is free and has many functions.
d. _____ Some people include negative personal information about themselves on MySpace.

Reading

CD 1:
Track 20

Modern Social Networking

Badoo   Geni   My Yearbook

Last.fm   Experience project   Library Thing

classmates   Facebook

Toilter   Shelfari

Bebo   Reunion

Hi 5

Friendster   Friend Reunited   haioo

Biip   Cloob   My Space   Foto log

[1] Throughout history, humans have had an urge to make social connections. Making friends is something that most people do naturally when meeting people through family and friends and getting to know people in their neighborhood, at school, or in the workplace. In addition, the Internet has introduced a new meeting place—the social networking site (SNS).

[2] Social networking sites were originally designed to help adults connect with other adults. Users developed their own profile containing personal information (such as likes and dislikes) which others could look through. When you found someone with similar interests to you that you wanted to contact, you posted a message and waited for a reply. These types of SNS were popular but **access** was usually **off limits** to children. It should come as no surprise that technologically savvy teenagers would want to use computers in a similar way.

[3] In the United States, MySpace.com is one of the largest social networking sites with over 100 million users. Unlike some sites that require a special invitation to join, MySpace is open to everyone over the age of 14. Users create their own personal profile page and can spend their time blogging, posting photos and instant messaging with other members from all over the world. They can then decide whether they want to make their profile available only to friends or to all registered users.

[4] Many teens now prefer using SNS to stay in touch with friends and meet new people. Instead of asking for a phone number or email address, asking for someone's MySpace profile is becoming a much more popular question. For many, these sites have made a positive difference in their lives by widening their social circles. However, some people have found social networking sites carry some risks. There are stories of employers offering a job and then changing their mind after checking the person's personal profile on the Internet. So be warned— it is important to think about the type of information you include on your profile page.

Comprehension Check

1 The word "access" in paragraph 2 is closest in meaning to:

a. entry   **b.** approach   **c.** route   **d.** exit

2 The phrase "off limits" in paragraph 2 is closest in meaning to:

a. not available   **b.** out of order   **c.** allowed   **d.** restricted

3 In paragraph 3, the author mentions MySpace.com as an example of:

a. A social networking site available to all ages.
b. A social networking site that teenagers may use.
c. A social networking site that employers use.
d. A social networking site that teenagers have created.

4 In paragraph 4, the author implies that employers use social networking sites to:

a. Increase the number of staff.   **b.** Fire staff who cause problems at work.
c. Find new staff.   **d.** Find out if someone is telling the truth.

5 Which of the following is NOT a feature of a social networking site mentioned in the text?

a. Meeting new people.   **b.** Communicatings with others.
c. Sharing information about yourself.   **d.** Finding a job.

More Word Chunks

1 Look at Clara's personal profile from a social networking site. Complete the profile by using these word chunks from Units 4, 5, and 6.

better than	friends	the world
something different	grades	time

Interests:
- Spending _____ **with family and** _____.
- Traveling **all over** _____.
- **Getting good** _____ in my university classes.

Hi, my name is Clara. Right after college, I got an office job working behind a desk. It was OK but after a few years I wanted to **do** _____ with my life. I wanted a job that allowed me to do what I loved, which is traveling. The only way to do this was to go back to school. I am now studying to get a degree in tourism. Once I graduate, I hope to get a job that's **much** _____ my old one. If you have some recommendations for countries to visit, let me know.

2 Underline the word which does NOT collocate with the word in bold.

a. get:	funny	married	home
b. have:	a big heart	a talent	an intelligence
c. look:	around	through	by
d. take:	a favor	me by surprise	your time

Here are some other word chunks made from "get", "has", and "take."

get:	upset	angry
have:	a good sense of humor	something in common with each other
take:	a nap	care of each other

3 Complete the sentences using any of the word chunks from this page.

a. Sometimes couples who **have nothing** _____ have surprisingly good relationships.

b. Some die-hard sports fans **get** _____ if their team loses, but they don't stay depressed for long.

c. When choosing a career, it is important that you **take** _____ to think about your interests and learn about careers related to those interests.

d. Many people who go on a volunteer vacation **have a** _____ and enjoy helping others.

e. Billy Mills **had** _____ for running.

f. Some MySpace members can spend hours **looking** _____ the personal profiles available on the website.

7 Finding Love

Warm Up

1 What is the best way for these people to find love? Tell a partner.

A

B

C

D

a.	_____	At a dance club.	b.	_____ Through friends.
c.	_____	On the Internet.	d.	_____ Through a dating agency.
e.	_____	At work/school.	f.	_____ Through family.
g.	_____	On vacation.	h.	_____ Through a newspaper/magazine advertisement.

2 What is the best way for you to find love? Rank the different ways above, from 1 (the best for you) to 8 (the worst way for you).

Reading Strategy: Making judgments

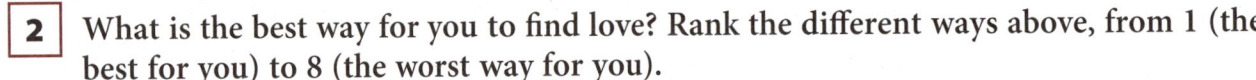

When you **judge** something, you decide if it is good or bad, right or wrong, interesting or boring, fair or unfair, strange or normal, etc. For example,

"When I was sixteen, I wanted to date a girl in my class because she had beautiful eyes and a cute nose. I didn't know anything else about her, but I thought I was in love with her."

Do you think the writer's reasons for falling in love with the girl were good reasons or bad reasons? Do you think his feelings are normal or unusual for a 16-year-old? Do you think he will be successful in finding love?
It is not important how you answer these questions, but it is important that you judge what you read. You can base your judgments on your own knowledge, your personal experience, as well as your opinions and reasoning. At school or college you need to make judgments all the time, whenever you write an essay, hold a discussion, or attend a lecture.

Strategy in Focus

1   Read the headline of this news story and look at the photo. Decide if you agree [✓] or disagree [×] with these judgments. Then compare your judgments with a partner.

a. _____ The woman is too old to get married.

b. _____ This must be true love.

c. _____ The man doesn't love the woman.

2   Now read the news story. Decide if you agree [✓] or disagree [×] with these judgments. Then compare your judgments with your partner.

a. _____ Muhamad and Wook will be very happy together.

b. _____ Being married 21 times is not normal.

c. _____ There must be another reason for Muhamad to marry Wook.

d. _____ This story is not interesting enough to be published in a newspaper.

33-Year-Old Marries 104-Year-Old

In Malaysia, a 33-year-old man married a 104-year-old woman, saying their respect for each other and friendship turned to love.

Local newspapers reported it was Muhamad Noor Che Musa's first marriage and his wife's 21st. According to The Star newspaper, Muhamad said, "I am not after her money, as she is poor. Her only asset is her deep religious knowledge. Through her I can deepen my knowledge of religion."

He also said that many people did not understand his decision to marry Wook Kundor. Some people have said their marriage is strange and have questioned his reasons for marrying a woman 71 years older than himself. However, Muhamad says that he has found peace and happiness since marrying Wook.

Feedback:

Here are some possible judgments for activity 2. Your ideas may be different.

a. The marriage will be difficult because of the age difference.

b. Marrying 21 times is not normal. People may think there is something strange or suspicious about Wook.

c. When there is a big age difference, few people will believe the couple is in love. People may think Muhamad is marrying for money, and Wook is marrying because she is lonely.

d. Marrying 21 times and marrying someone so much older / younger is a story that would interest many people.

Parents Know Best

Before Reading

1 Look at the title of the text and the photo. What do you think the story is about?

    a. Parents are more intelligent than their children.

    b. Parents know how to educate their children better than teachers.

    c. Sometimes parents can choose a good husband or wife for their children.

2 Read the first and second sentence of the text and check your hypothesis.

While Reading

3 As you read each paragraph, decide if you agree [✓] or disagree [✗] with these judgments.

Paragraph 1:

a. _____ Naresh is too young to get married.

b. _____ Naresh should find a wife by himself.

c. _____ Asking your parents to find your wife or husband is a good idea.

d. _____ Naresh and Priya have a good chance of a successful marriage.

Paragraph 2:

a. _____ You should know someone for a long time before you get married.

b. _____ Before marrying someone, it is important to know he/she comes from a good family.

c. _____ Arranged marriages cannot work in my country.

d. _____ An arranged marriage would work for me.

Paragraph 3:

a. _____ Arranged marriages only work in India because of their traditions.

b. _____ Arranged marriages in India stop young people from making mistakes.

c. _____ If there were more arranged marriages in the world, there would be fewer divorces.

d. _____ Love is not important when deciding to get married.

After Reading

4 Compare your judgments with a partner.

5 What inferences can you make? Write "Yes," "No" or "Maybe."

    a. Naresh only wanted to marry an Indian girl. _____

    b. Naresh didn't like any of the 40 women his parents found. _____

    c. Priya agreed to meet Naresh because she liked his picture. _____

    d. Naresh and Priya couldn't meet until their families agreed. _____

    e. Naresh and Priya have been married for at least seven years. _____

    f. Nowadays, most people in India have arranged marriages. _____

CD 2: Track 1

Parents Know Best

[1] When Naresh Kumar was 28, he called his parents with an important request. He was ready to marry and he wanted his parents to find him a wife. Since he was living in Canada, he wanted a wife who would move to North America and could speak English. After two months of searching, Naresh's parents found forty potential wives. They sent pictures and resumes to Naresh, and he chose Priya, a woman from the same town as his family.

[2] Priya had just finished college in India, and her parents were also trying to find a husband for her. When Priya saw Naresh's picture and read his personal resume, she became interested. They had many things in common and she thought they could be a good match. After both families had checked each other out, Naresh and Priya finally met in person. Priya and Naresh both wanted to know if their parents had forced the other into the marriage. They were glad to find out that they had both asked their parents to help arrange a marriage. The system of arranged marriage worked well for them as they are now happily married with two seven-year-old sons.

[3] Arranged marriages are common in India, so it doesn't seem strange for parents to help their children find a husband or wife. Rather, children trust their parents to know what is best for their future. Also, because dating is not very common in India, marriage is seen as the start of a relationship, and love grows during a marriage.

Word Work

6 **Complete the sentences with a word chunk from the text.**

finished college	have many things in common	happily married	met in person

a. My parents didn't want me to get married until I had _____.

b. My best friend in high school and I _____. We like the same music, movies, and fashion.

c. I have been chatting with this girl on the Internet for a year. We _____ last night, but we didn't like each other.

d. My parents have been _____ for more than 30 years, and they never fight.

Finding Love in the 21st Century

Before Reading

1   How do you think Americans find love these days? Choose one or more answers.
   a. Through the Internet.
   b. Through family and friends.
   c. Through their hobbies, e.g., book clubs, playing sport.
   d. Through a matchmaker (a person you pay to find a husband/wife for you).
   e. Through special dating events for single people, e.g., speed dates.
   f. At work.

2   Read the first paragraph to check your hypotheses.

While Reading

3   As you read the news story, decide what the writer is saying, about the following:
   a. ". . . matchmakers are a thing of the past" (line 9)
      i.   Matchmaking is no longer popular.   **ii.** Matchmaking has a long tradition.
   b. ". . . the Internet is an affordable option." (line 17).
      i.   Online dating is the most expensive option.   **ii.** Online dating isn't expensive.
   c. ". . . there are many ways to meet the love of your life" (line 33).
      i.   You can find a partner in a variety of ways.   **ii.** You can love life in a variety of ways.

After Reading

4   Decide if you agree [✓] or disagree [✗] with these judgments. Then compare your ideas with a partner.
   a. _____ Charging people to find a husband or wife is a good idea for a business.
   b. _____ It is unnatural to find love through the Internet or a matchmaker.
   c. _____ Americans should spend more time to find love on their own.
   d. _____ It is better to find love through an Internet dating service than to pay for an expensive matchmaker.
   e. _____ Speed dating is the best way to find a partner.

5   Decide if the statements are true (**T**) or false (**F**), according to the text.
   a.   **T**   **F**   Many Americans are finding love by meeting people through work and family.
   b.   **T**   **F**   Some people in New York pay matchmakers $16,000 to find love for them.
   c.   **T**   **F**   Online daters meet 20 people for three minutes each and exchange email addresses.
   d.   **T**   **F**   Single people looking for love can go on special holidays and to dinner parties.

Finding Love in the 21st Century

Helping people find love is becoming big business in America. Online dating services, special events for single people, and matchmakers are turning love into a billion dollar industry. After [5] trying and failing at the traditional way of finding love in America—meeting people through work, hobbies, family or friends—many Americans are gladly paying top dollar to find love.

You may think matchmakers are a thing of the [10] past, but not in many American cities. Top matchmakers in New York can charge $16,000 to find the perfect match for their clients. In one year, a few matchmakers can earn as much as $5 million, and they often receive a bonus when [15] clients get married. A bonus may be more money, jewelry, or even a new car.

For people who cannot pay a matchmaker, the Internet is an affordable option. Online dating services allow users to post an ad for a small monthly fee. [20] Users can look through other personal ads, choose potential partners, and then email them. After getting to know each other through email, online daters can then decide if they want to meet in person. According to some reports, 40 million Americans use online [25] dating services each month.

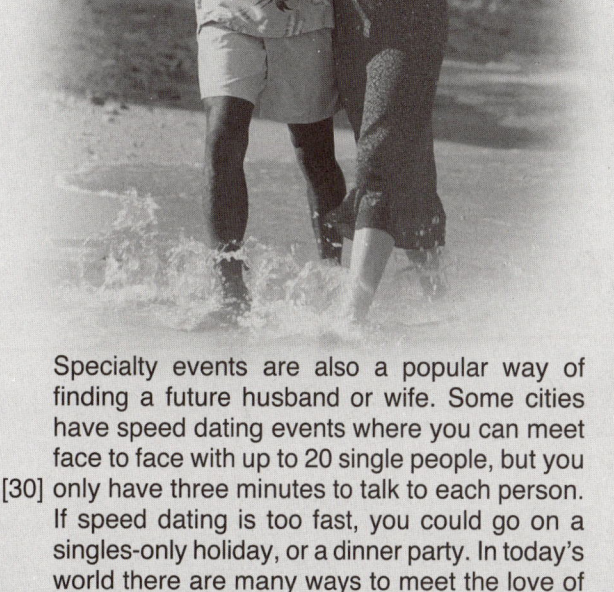

Specialty events are also a popular way of finding a future husband or wife. Some cities have speed dating events where you can meet face to face with up to 20 single people, but you [30] only have three minutes to talk to each person. If speed dating is too fast, you could go on a singles-only holiday, or a dinner party. In today's world there are many ways to meet the love of your life, but they aren't all free.

Word Work

6 Complete the word chunks in the paragraph below with words from the box.

| to get married | face to face | match | to know each other | in person |

Although there are many ways to find love, people around the world follow a similar process to help them **find their perfect** _____. First of all, it is important that a couple **get** _____ so they can find out if they have things in common. In some countries, the couple will **speak** _____. In other countries, the couple may **meet** _____ and then set up a date at a restaurant or the movies. Then, if the date is successful, the couple will spend more time together. Finally, after they have got to know each other, they can decide if they **want** _____.

Before Reading

1 Take one minute to scan the text to find the answers.

 a. What are the names of the writer's parents? _____
 b. Where did the writer's parents meet? _____
 c. How did the writer's parents meet? _____

2 How do you think the writer feels about the way her parents met?

 a. embarrassed **b.** happy **c.** upset **d.** sad **e.** ashamed

While Reading

3 As you are reading the text, decide if the writer's mother and father were good friends to Peter.

After Reading

4 Tell a partner your ideas from activity 3.

5 Decide if you agree [✓] or disagree [✗] with these judgments. Then compare your judgments with your partner.

 a. _____ It was wrong of Martha to date someone she wasn't really interested in.
 b. _____ It was OK for Archie to sing a love song to his friend's date.
 c. _____ It was good that Martha paid attention to Peter the rest of the night.
 d. _____ It was good that Martha called Peter to ask for Archie's number.

6 Match the first part of the sentence to the second part.

 a. At the beginning of the story, •   • **i.** was the one.
 b. Martha didn't think that Peter •   • **ii.** Archie's phone number.
 c. Peter's friend was singing •   • **iii.** Martha was dating Peter.
 d. Archie dedicated a song •   • **iv.** at a nightclub.
 e. Martha asked Peter for •   • **v.** to the writer's mom.

CD 2: Track 3

A Nightclub Romance

Before my mom, Martha, met my dad, she dated a guy named Peter. She knew that Peter wasn't "the one"—the man she wanted to marry—but she enjoyed his company and they had fun [5] hanging out with each other. One day Peter asked Martha if she wanted to go to Ziggy's, a nightclub where a friend of his was singing. She thought that would be fun and agreed to go.

When they arrived at the nightclub, Peter found [10] his friend, Archie, and introduced him to my mom. In an instant, Martha was taken by the tall, attractive guy. He reminded her of Tony Bennett, a famous singer in the 1950s and 60s, whom she really liked. They all chatted for a [15] while and then it was Archie's time to sing.

Martha expected Archie to begin by introducing himself and then singing some of his songs. She couldn't believe it when he opened his act with, "I'd like to dedicate this song to that beautiful [20] woman sitting over there," and he pointed at Martha. The song he sang was the love song,

If I loved you. Martha didn't know what to do. This attractive, talented man was singing to her, [25] right in front of his friend. She glanced at Peter who looked upset and jealous.

Martha decided that the right thing to do was ignore Archie and pay attention to Peter for the rest of the night. After Archie finished, she and [30] Peter left the club to go out to dinner. Peter didn't talk about what had happened and she decided not to mention it.

However, over the next few days, Martha couldn't stop thinking about Archie. She knew she wanted [35] to see him again but she didn't know his phone number or where he was singing next. The only way to find him was to ask Peter. Eventually, she called Peter up and asked for Archie's number—which I'm glad she did, or I wouldn't [40] be telling this story today!

Word Work

7 Use these word chunks to complete the sentences.

right in front of	couldn't stop thinking about
couldn't believe it	the right thing to do

a. Martha _____ when Archie started singing to her.

b. Martha was amazed that Archie would sing a love song to her _____ his friend, Peter.

c. She thought that _____ was to pay attention to Peter.

d. At the end of the story, Martha decided to call Archie because she _____ him.

Reflection

▶ Which was your favorite text in this unit? Why?

▶ Which reading strategies did you use in this unit?

▶ Which new word chunks will you make an effort to use in the next five days? Choose at least five.

8 Kindness

Warm Up

1 | Which of these acts of kindness have you done in the last four weeks?

  a. Phoned someone you haven't spoken to in a long time to say "hello".
  b. Smiled and said "hello" to someone you don't know.
  c. Picked up litter.
  d. Opened a door for someone.
  e. Visited an elderly neighbor who has no family nearby.
  f. Offered to carry someone's heavy shopping bags.
  g. Offered to babysit for free.
  h. Volunteered to help younger students study at a school.
  i. Donated blood.
  j. Complimented someone.

2 | What was your most generous act of kindness? Tell a partner.

Reading Strategy: Making associations

There are a number of ways good readers think about the text while they are reading. Good readers think about similar situations from **their own lives** and **associate** the text with their own personal knowledge.

For example, when reading, the sentence, "It was the night before Lisa's final English exam, she was tired and drinking a lot of coffee." readers may think about a similar experience they had. They may think about:

- Where they were studying for their English exam.
- Why they were still studying late.
- How they felt while they were studying.
- What happened in the exam (if they passed or failed).

Readers may also think about their personal knowledge of things connected to the text:

- examinations, such as TOEIC® and TOEFL®.
- the effects of drinking coffee.
- the benefits of studying the night before an examination.

It is important to **connect the text to your experiences** and **make associations**. It can help you understand a situation described in the text more fully.

Strategy in Focus

As you are reading the story *Cold Hands, Warm Heart*, ask a partner the following questions about the text.

Cold Hands, Warm Heart

It was a very cold winter, and I was outside running some errands for my mother.
  a. How cold is the winter in your hometown?
  b. What errands do you run for your family or friends?
  c. Do you prefer to be indoors or outside in the winter?

On the way back to our warm apartment, I saw an old homeless woman. She was dressed in a thin jacket and was begging for spare change.
  d. Are there homeless people in your country?
  e. Where do they stay? How do they get food?

I was a student and broke so I had no money to give her. Yet this old woman was blue with cold and I felt bad not giving her anything. I realized that there was something I could do to help her.
  f. Have you ever been in a situation where you had no money?
  g. When was the last time you were blue with cold?
  h. Have you ever given homeless people money?

I went over to her, pulled off my warm gloves and put them on her hands. I said that I was sorry for not giving any money and that I hoped the gloves would help. The old woman smiled and quietly thanked me.
  i. What did you do the last time you saw a homeless person?
  j. Have you heard or read about any stories about homeless people?

Feedback:

The text is about a student helping a homeless woman. The questions should make you think about similar situations that you have experienced and what you know about homeless people.

An Apple a Day

Before Reading

1 Think about the times when you have been kind or helped someone. How did it make you feel? Choose one or more answers.

tired	more relaxed	stronger	healthier
happy	sad	stressed	peaceful

2 Skim the text. What is the main idea?

  a. Healthy people are kind because they have more energy.
  b. Kind people can be stressed because they are always helping.
  c. Doing kind things can make you feel good and help you be healthier.

While Reading

3 As you read the text, check your hypothesis. Underline any statements that confirm your answer.

After Reading

4 Relate the text to your personal experiences. Answers these questions.

  a. Do you have an expression like "an apple a day keeps the doctor away" in your first language?
  b. Other than acts of kindness, what activities help you feel calm and less stressed?
  c. Do you think you would experience "helper's high" if you volunteered your time?
  d. Can you describe a time you were stressed, or felt depressed?
  e. What raises your self-esteem and makes you feel optimistic?

5 Choose the correct ending to complete the statements.

  a. According to the article:
   i.   it is better to be kind than eat well.
   ii. kindness can help you feel healthy.
  b. You can get a helper's high:
   i.   by volunteering your time.
   ii. by taking painkillers.
  c. The study found that people who help others can have:
   i.   sleeping problems and stress.
   ii. fewer health problems.
  d. Another study of almost 3,000 men showed that people who volunteered:
   i.   lived longer.
   ii. wanted to live longer.

An Apple a Day

There is a saying, "An apple a day keeps the doctor away." Although eating properly is important, being kind to others is also good for your health. Studies show that people who
[5] perform kind acts are more relaxed, happier, and healthier than other people.

In one study at Arizona State University, researchers found that many volunteers experienced a sudden feeling of joy, followed
[10] by a long period of calm, after performing a kind act. This feeling, called "a helper's high," may actually help reduce stress as the body releases natural painkillers.

Stress can cause serious health problems, and
[15] can lead to high blood pressure and heart disease. Stress can also lead to overeating, depression, and sleeping problems. However, the study found that volunteers had fewer stress-related health problems when they did helpful
[20] things for other people.

The study also found that people who did nice things for others felt better about themselves as well. They had higher self-esteem, and were happier. Many believe this is because volunteers
[25] spend more of their time with other people. People who are more outgoing are often healthier.

Another study at the University of Michigan's Survey Research Center confirmed the health benefits of volunteering. A ten-year study of
[30] 2,700 men in Michigan showed that people who volunteered lived longer than those who didn't. Although you shouldn't need a reason to be helpful, it is nice to know that kindness may help you live longer.

Word Work

6 Circle the correct word to complete the word chunk.

a. Doctors tell us that **eating properly / eating correctly** will help us be happy and healthy.

b. Many **studies present / studies show** that exercise and a healthy diet can help prevent obesity.

c. If you **perform a kind act / do a kind act**, you can help someone and feel good about yourself.

d. Depression and overeating are often **stress-caused / stress-related**.

e. If you volunteer your time to help other people, it could help you **have higher self-esteem / bigger self-esteem**.

Teaching Kindness

Before Reading

1 **Read the beginning of the text below and predict what will happen next.**

Chuck Wall teaches management and human relations at Bakersfield College. He walked into class one day and told his students that their homework was to ...

a. write an essay about kindness.
b. be kind to a stranger.
c. find a charity and volunteer their time.

While Reading

2 **As you read the text, decide if you agree [✓] or disagree [✗] with these judgments.**

a. _____ Chuck Wall is an unusual teacher.
b. _____ The students all chose very difficult homework assignments.
c. _____ Chuck Wall's homework assignment would be good idea for my class.

After Reading

3 **Imagine your homework assignment was to do a random act of kindness. Tell a partner what you would do.**

4 **What did you think about in each paragraph? Which of these ideas did you have? Write "Yes" or "No."**

Paragraph		Yes/No
1	a. A strange homework assignment my teacher gave me.	
	b. A time I didn't understand my teachers' directions.	
	c. I don't like to do homework.	
2	a. A class you were excited about.	
	b. A time when you were kind.	
	c. A time when someone was kind to you.	
3	a. If your school should celebrate Kindness Day on November 13th.	
	b. Kind things your school or students in your school already do.	
	c. Charities you would like your school to raise money for.	

5 **Check [✓] the inferences you can make about the text.**

a. _____ The students didn't understand the homework immediately.
b. _____ The students got good grades in Chuck Wall's class.
c. _____ The students enjoyed doing the homework assignment.
d. _____ The students only helped people they knew.

6 **Underline the words, phrases, or sentences that support your inferences in activity 5.**

CD 2:
Track 5

Teaching Kindness

[1] Chuck Wall teaches management and human relations at Bakersfield College. He walked into class one day and told his students that their homework was to perform one act of random kindness. His students did not understand the assignment, but the professor would not answer their questions. He encouraged his students to figure it out for themselves.

[2] One week later, the students entered the classroom excited to share their stories. One student told of distributing blankets to the homeless, another reported on helping a dog to find its owner, and another student had contacted a long, lost friend. Students were energized by the homework assignment and wanted other people to be kind too. With the support of local businesses, the students made stickers to put on cars that challenged people to do something kind for others. They sold the stickers and decided to donate the money to a center for the blind—not surprising as Professor Wall is blind.

[3] Since then, similar kindness campaigns have been started in schools around the world. Many schools organize a Random Acts of Kindness Week, around November 13th, to celebrate World Kindness Day. Some schools use each day of Random Acts of Kindness Week to perform a different kind act, such as making a new friend, helping someone, doing community service, or raising money for a charity. Students learn to consider other people and think about how small actions can make the world a better place.

Word Work

7 Complete the word chunks in the sentences below with words from the box.

| their stories | lost friend | for themselves | money to | money for |

a. The students were confused by the mathematics problem. They needed their teachers' help because they couldn't **figure it out** _____.

b. The students came back from an exciting summer vacation and couldn't wait to **share** _____ with their classmates.

c. Last year, our school decided to **raise** _____ children who needed help around the world. We made more than $6,000 and **donated the** _____ UNICEF.

d. **A long,** _____ is someone you have not seen or spoken to in many years.

Women Who Make a Difference

Before Reading

1 You are going to read about three women who are helping others. List some problems you have heard about (make associations).

a. Environmental problems: _____ _____
b. Social problems: _____ _____
c. Health problems: _____ _____

While Reading

2 As you read, underline the problems mentioned in the text.

After Reading

3 Which of the following did you think about while you were reading the text? Write "Yes" if you made the association or "No" if you didn't.

Phrase	Association	Yes/No
a. "improve the environment"	recycle paper, glass, and plastic	
b. "create important roles for women"	give women good jobs	
c. "supporting women's education"	give more scholarships to women.	
d. "education programs for poor families"	building schools	

4 Check [✓] the INCORRECT ending for each statement.

a. According to the article, The Green Belt Movement in Kenya:
  i. _____ helps Kenyan women find jobs.
  ii. _____ helps plant more trees in Kenyan forests.
  iii. _____ helps Kenyan farmers produce food.

b. According to the article, Queen Rania wants to:
  i. _____ help more women to read and write.
  ii. _____ protect the traditional roles of women.
  iii. _____ help children be healthier and better educated.

c. From the article we can infer that the Gates Foundation uses its money to:
  i. _____ give Internet access to poor people around the world.
  ii. _____ give poor communities access to doctors and medicine.
  iii. _____ provide books and teachers to poor communities.

CD 2:
Track 6

Women Who Make a Difference

One person can make a difference in the world—perhaps it is an act of kindness for one person or something that leads to major changes for a whole country. Wangari Maathai from Kenya,
[5] Queen Rania from Jordan, and Melinda Gates from the United States are three women who volunteer their time to make life better for whole populations.

Professor Maathai started The Green Belt Movement
[10] in Kenya which helps to improve the environment and create important roles for women. The movement aims to reduce the effects of deforestation and soil erosion, and provides an opportunity for women to be leaders. Since 1977, Kenyans have planted over
[15] 30 million trees. More importantly, communities are more aware of the relationship between the environment and other issues, such as health and food production. In 1994, Maathai was the first African woman to win a Nobel Peace Prize for her
[20] work and The Green Belt Movement is now an international organization.

Queen Rania of Jordan dedicates much of her time to supporting women's rights and education. Her message challenges traditional customs in an
[25] area of the world where more than 60 percent of women cannot read and write, and many women cannot vote. She often speaks about the benefits of involving women in the economic and political community because she believes a better society
[30] starts with the education of women.

Melinda Gates started the Gates Foundation with her husband, Microsoft's Bill Gates. This foundation gives money to education programs for poor families, and to global health projects
[35] to combat diseases such as HIV/AIDS, malaria, and tuberculosis. The Gates have already promised more than 29 billion dollars to develop educational programs and distribute medicine to communities around the world. The foundation
[40] is dedicated to making the world a healthier and better place for everyone.

Word Work

5 Match the words to make word chunks from the text. Then choose one word chunk and write a sentence about yourself.

a. volunteer •   • i.   life better
b. raising •   • ii. an opportunity
c. make •   • iii. your time
d. provides •   • iv. children

Reflection

▶ Which was your favorite text in this unit? Why?

▶ Which reading strategies did you use in this unit?

▶ Which new word chunks will you make an effort to use in the next five days? Choose at least five.

9 Bravery

Warm Up

1 Look at the pictures and rank them from 1 (bravest) to 6 (least brave).

A _____

B _____

C _____

D _____

E _____

F _____

2 Show your ranking to a partner and compare your answers.

Reading Strategy: Deducing the meaning of words from context

You can find words you don't understand when reading in your first language as well as your second language. However, you can't always use a dictionary to understand every word in a text. Often it is better to guess the meaning of words from the context—or situation—you find them in. This is called **deducing** (or guessing) **meaning from context**.

For example, what does the word valiantly mean in the sentence below?

"The brave firefighters tried valiantly to save the family's pet from the burning house."

    a. quietly
    b. bravely
    c. slowly

You would probably choose bravely, because firefighters are trying to save a pet in a house that is burning and this is a very dangerous thing to do. The correct answer must be b. as the firefighters are acting bravely.

Strategy in Focus

1   **Look at the picture. What do you think "toxic" means?**

   a. Very tasty.
   b. Very dangerous.
   c. Very spicy.

Feedback:

The correct answer is b. You should be able to guess that toxic means very dangerous because the label is telling you not to drink the liquid and has a symbol warning of danger.

2   **Look at the picture. What do you think "flammable" means?**

   a. Cannot catch fire easily.
   b. Can catch fire easily.
   c. Can get dirty easily.

Feedback:

The correct answer is b. You should be able to guess that flammable means "can catch fire easily" because the label is telling you not leave it near heat and has a symbol warning of fire.

3   **Guess the meaning of the bold words in these sentences.**

   a. The birds are **soaring** above the clouds. They look like small airplanes.
     i. making a noise   **ii.** flying high   **iii.** feeling scared
   b. Sam Jones received a medal of **valor** from the mayor for running into a burning building and saving the lives of two children.
     i. bravery   **ii.** cowardice   **iii.** weakeness.
   c. Jane makes friends wherever she goes because of her **gregarious** personality.
     i. outgoing   **ii.** shy   **iii.** aggressive

Feedback:

   a. The correct answer is ii. The sentence is about birds, and birds fly. Also, soaring is a verb and the birds are doing this above the clouds, so they must be flying high.
   b. The correct answer is i. Someone who risks his or her life to run into a burning building is brave. A medal of valor recognizes an act of bravery.
   c. The correct answer is i. People like Jane and she makes friends easily.

Before Reading

1 Check [✓] the words that you associate with surfing.

_____ flowers _____ beach _____ surfboard _____ ocean
_____ sharks _____ Hawaii _____ lake _____ wave

2 Write any other words you associate with surfing.

3 Look at the title of the article and the photo. What do you think the text is about?

While Reading

4 As you read the text, check your hypothesis. Decide if you want to change your hypothesis.

After Reading

5 Ask a partner these questions about the text.
   a. Is Bethany Hamilton brave or crazy to continue surfing?
   b. Would you continue surfing after a shark attack?

6 Find the underlined words in the text. Then circle the meaning of each word.
   a. When something is <u>attacked</u>, it is **hurt by something / touched gently**.
   b. If something is <u>applied</u>, it is **taken off / put on**.
   c. A <u>tourniquet</u> is a **bathing suit / bandage**.
   d. When you <u>head to</u> something, you **go to a destination / swim**.
   e. <u>Numerous</u> means **one / many**.
   f. If someone is <u>disabled</u>, they have a **physical challenge / special talent**.
   g. When you <u>overcome adversity</u>, you beat **your team / problems**.

7 Decide if the statements are true (**T**) or false (**F**).
   a. T F Bethany Hamilton was a very good surfer before the shark attack.
   b. T F Bethany was close to the beach when she was attacked.
   c. T F Bethany's friend was also attacked.
   d. T F It took Bethany a long time to recover from the attack.
   e. T F Bethany's career as a surfer is over.
   f. T F Bethany only surfs where there are no sharks.
   g. T F Bethany gives a lot of inspiring speeches around the world.

CD 2:
Track 7

Riding the Wave

Bethany Hamilton, a 13-year-old champion surfer, was in the water waiting for the next wave. It was a beautiful morning in Hawaii and she was surfing with her best friend, Alana, and her friend's father.

[5] Bethany was lying on her surfboard with her left arm hanging in the water when she felt something grab it. Suddenly she saw the blood and realized a shark had attacked her.

The shark swam off with Bethany's arm while [10] Bethany called to the others that she needed to get back to shore—a 15-minute swim. Alana's father quickly came over, applied a tourniquet to stop the bleeding, and the group headed to the beach. Luckily, Bethany made it to the [15] hospital in time to save her life.

Most people would probably stop surfing after a shark attack, but Bethany was determined to continue. Ten weeks after the attack, she competed in a surfing event and placed fifth. [20] She has since entered numerous competitions and has even placed first in a few of them.

Bethany only goes into the water when sharks are not feeding, but she still sees sharks. How does she remain calm? Singing and trying to [25] focus on having fun and surfing. Although Bethany is busy with school and surfing, she makes time to help raise money for disabled children around the world. For her courage and positive attitude, Bethany has received numerous [30] awards and she uses her story to inspire others to overcome adversity.

Word Work

8 **Correct the mistakes in these word chunks.**

a. I overslept this morning but luckily my mother woke me up and I **made it to school at time** for the exam. _____

b. A man was choking in the restaurant, but someone **rescued his life**.

_____

c. My teacher tells me to **remain relaxed** during a test but I always get nervous.

_____

d. My father is a very busy man, but he always **does time** to help me with my homework.

_____

e. My class decided to **build money** for a children's hospital in our town. _____

_____

Before Reading

1 Look at the photo. What do you think the text is about? Choose one or more answers.

a. Going to school.   **b.** A child leader.   **c.** A child worker.

d. Having a hobby.   **e.** Learning to make something.   **f.** Unsafe working conditions.

While Reading

2 As you read, decide if you want to change your hypothesis.

After Reading

3 Ask a partner these questions about the text.

a. Where could you find out more information about the Bonded Labor Liberation Front?

b. Do you think Iqbal Masih was brave? Why?

4 Choose the best definition of the words in bold. Look at the surrounding words to help you guess the meaning.

a. They may work in a family business or do **odd jobs** like babysitting. (line 4)

    i. strange and difficult work

    ii. work that you sometimes do to make a little money

    iii. full-time employment

b. As a **bonded** child **laborer** in Pakistan, he had no freedom, and had to do everything his owner told him. (line 9)

    i. a worker who is owned by someone and must work for them

    ii. a worker who makes a lot of money

    iii. a manager of a factory

c. He was **malnourished** because he wasn't fed properly, and he was often beaten by his owners. (line 12)

    i. unhealthy because of a poor diet

    ii treated badly

    iii. healthy

d. Iqbal was inspired to speak that day and gave a **moving speech** about his terrible life. He was a natural speaker, and his impressive and touching speech caught the attention of BLLF. (line 19)

    i. a boring speech

    ii. a speech that encourages people to move somewhere new

    iii. an emotional and memorable speech

CD 2:
Track 8

Small but Powerful

Although most people expect to work when they finish school or college, there are a number of children who work at an early age. They may work in a family business or do odd jobs like [5] babysitting. However, some children are forced to work and some are even sold to raise money for their family.

Iqbal Masih was four years old when his father sold him. As a bonded child laborer in Pakistan, [10] he had no freedom, and had to do everything his owner told him. Iqbal worked in the carpet industry, toiling for 16 hours a day. He was malnourished because he wasn't fed properly, and he was often beaten by his owners.

[15] When Iqbal was ten, he attended a freedom day celebration organized by the Bonded Labor Liberation Front (BLLF). He learned about his rights and found out that he could demand his freedom.

Iqbal was inspired to speak that day and gave a [20] moving speech about his terrible life. He was a natural speaker, and his impressive and touching speech caught the attention of BLLF.

With the help of the BLLF, Iqbal received his freedom and joined the organization. Traveling [25] around Pakistan, he talked to children about their rights and helped to free over 3,000 children. Iqbal also traveled to other countries around the world, raising international awareness of the carpet industry and its working conditions.

[30] Iqbal, an intelligent boy, was determined to become a lawyer and spend his life helping bonded children. Sadly, when he was 12, he was assassinated. Many believe the Pakistani carpet "mafia" killed him. Although his life was short, Iqbal's message to end child labor is still being heard around the world.

Word Work

5 | **Complete the sentences with one of these word chunks from the text.**

> spend his life   at an early age   determined to become   to raise awareness

a. John trained in the gym all day because he was _____ a professional athlete.

b. Many celebrities use their fame _____ of different problems around the world, such as poverty and hunger.

c. Steve didn't want to _____ working in an office, so he started his own gardening business.

d. Mozart could play the piano like an adult _____ .

Before Reading

1 Look at the pictures below and guess what the story is about.

a. Three people who save other people's lives.
b. A father who tests his three sons.
c. Three detectives looking for a criminal.

While Reading

2 Read the first paragraph and check your hypothesis.

3 Read the rest of the story and put the pictures in order.

  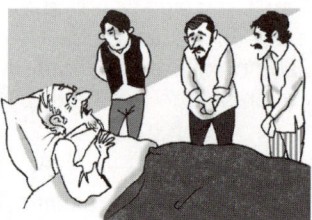 

A _____ B _____ C _____ D _____

After Reading

4 Ask a partner these questions about the text.

a. Do you think the father made the right decision?
b. Who do you think is the most generous person? Why?

5 Find these words in the story and work out their meaning.

a. gathered (line 14)
   i. met   **ii.** talked

b. drowning (line 23)
   i. die under water   **ii.** die from falling from a high building

c. on the edge (line 31)
   i. close to the end of the cliff   **ii.** far from the end of the cliff

d. enemy (line 36)
   i. friend   **ii.** opponent

e. dragged (line 37)
   i. moved easily   **ii.** moved with difficulty

f. swore (line 40)
   i. promised   **ii.** spoke impolitely

CD 2:
Track 9

A True Hero

There once was a poor father who lived with his three sons. The father was very old and knew that he would die soon. The only thing he owned of value was a diamond, but he couldn't [5] decide who to give it to because he loved all his sons the same.

One day, he called his sons to his bedroom and said, "Sons, as you know, the only valuable thing I have is a diamond. I do not want to sell [10] it, but I cannot choose who to give it to. So, I have decided to give the diamond to the son who does the greatest good. Return in one week and tell me what good things you have done."

After a week, the sons all gathered together [15] again at the father's bed. "Oldest son, tell me what good deed you did," the old man said.

The oldest son told his father that he had given half of everything he owned to the poor people in their city. The father thought this was good but [20] not good enough because everyone should help the poor.

The second son told him how he saved a little girl who was drowning in the river. Although the son wasn't a good swimmer, he had risked his [25] own life to save the child. The father thought this was better but everyone should do what they can to save a child.

"Now, what have you done, my youngest child?" the old man asked.

[30] The third son began to tell his story. One day while walking, he saw a man sleeping on the edge of a cliff. If the man rolled the wrong way, he would fall over the cliff. The son decided to go to the man and move him away from the cliff. When he got [35] closer, he realized that the man was Sancho, his enemy, a man who had promised to kill him. Yet, the youngest son decided to help him and dragged him away from the cliff. When Sancho awoke, he couldn't believe that he had been saved and the [40] two men swore to be friends.

The father was very proud of this last act. "You are truly kind. Few people would do something to save their enemy. I will give you the diamond."

Word Work

6 **Use three of these word chunks from the story to write sentences about yourself, your family or your friends.**

elderly father	gathered together	a poor man	the youngest child
is proud of	risked his own life	tell his story	on the edge of a cliff

a. _____

b. _____

c. _____

Reflection

▶ Which was your favorite text in this unit? Why?

▶ Which reading strategies did you use in this unit?

▶ Which new word chunks will you make an effort to use in the next five days? Choose at least five.

Review Reading Strategies

- Unit 7: Making judgments
- Unit 8: Making associations
- Unit 9: Deducing the meaning of words from context

1 Which reading strategies do these sentences describe? Read each statement and check [✓] the best answer.

	Making Judgments	Making Associations	Deducing Meaning
a. Think about something that happened in your own life that is similar to something in the text.			
b. Decide if a person in the text is good or bad.			
c. Think about the situation in the text to understand new words.			
d. Decide if you agree or disagree with an opinion in the text.			
e. Decide if you think the text is interesting.			
f. Think about something you know that is connected to the text.			
g. Decide if you want to finish reading the text.			
h. Decide if you want to recommend the text to a friend.			

2 Read the text and decide if you agree [✓] or disagree [×] with these judgments. Then compare your judgments with a partner.

a. _____ The honeybee is more important than I thought it was.

b. _____ There would be a serious problem if the honeybee disappeared.

c. _____ It is important for people to understand the honeybees' role in agriculture.

3 Write a check [✓] if you thought about these things when you read the text or a cross [×] if you didn't. Tell a partner what you thought about.

a. _____ bee stings   **b.** _____ eating honey

c. _____ plants, flowers, and fields you have seen   **d.** _____ farmers and farms

4 Match the words from the text with their synonyms. Deduce the meaning of each word from its context in the text.

a. key role   •
b. sole producer   •
c. crops   •
d. affordable   •

  • **i.** harvest, farmer's product such as cotton, corn, or rice
  • **ii.** important part
  • **iii.** not expensive
  • **iv.** only person/thing making something

Reading

CD 2: Track 10

More Than Honey

[1] The honeybee plays a key role in both the natural and human world. However, most people do not understand how important the honeybee is to our society. Many mistakenly assume that bees are only useful for making honey. In addition to being the sole producer of honey, the honeybee plays a vital part in our ecological and economic world.

[2] Without the honeybee, there would probably be fewer and less variety of plants in our world. For new and different plants to grow, they need to create seeds. Seeds are created when pollen (the white or yellow powder that flowers and plants produce) is moved from one plant to another. Insects, like the bee, are important because they help to move pollen from plant to plant. Pollen has to be transferred in order for the plants to reproduce. This is called pollination. When pollination doesn't happen, plants cannot reproduce and their numbers decrease.

[3] In addition to this ecological value, the honeybee provides a key economic service to the agricultural business which also depends on pollination. In the United States, the honeybee has become a primary source of pollination for crops. Many farmers will raise honeybees to make sure that their crops are being pollinated. Thanks to the honeybee, many farmers are able to produce large quantities of fruits and vegetables. As a result of the honeybees' work, people can continue to buy healthy food at an affordable price. Without question, the honeybee has made our life, and our diet, much better.

[4] The impact that the honeybee has on our life is amazing. Not only does it do a valuable job in creating food crops for the world, it also helps the environment by playing its part in creating many different plants.

Comprehension Check

1   The word "producer" in paragraph 1 is closest in meaning to:

    a. farmer   **b.** maker   **c.** grower   **d.** honeybee

2   The word "vital" in paragraph 1 is closest in meaning to:

    a. interesting   **b.** good   **c.** living   **d.** necessary

3   The author gives "pollination" in paragraph 2 as an example of the honeybee's importance to:

    a. the ecological world   **b.** the insect world

    c. farmers   **d.** honey producers

4   The author mentions the United States in paragraph 3 because:

    a. Only the United States benefits from honeybees.

    b. Farmers use honeybees to pollinate and produce more crops.

    c. In the USA, agriculture depends on pollination.

    d. The United States needs honeybees in order to produce honey.

5   Which statement best expresses the author's opinion of the honeybee?

    a. They are useful for farmers.

    b. They are an interesting insect for scientists to study.

    c. They are an important and helpful insect for the whole world.

    d. Their greatest contribution is honey.

More Word Chunks

1   Complete the sentences using these word chunks from the text and Units 7, 8, and 9.

spends its life	raise awareness of	eat properly
make our lives better	changed my mind	as a result of

    a. I used to be afraid of bees and thought they were useless. However, after reading how important they are, I've _____.

    b. Naomi Watts, the Hollywood actress, has been a special representative of the United Nations for HIV/AIDS since 2006. Her job is to _____ the dangers of HIV/AIDS around the world.

    c. Because of honeybees, farmers are able to produce a lot of fruits and vegetables. _____ the honeybee's work, people can buy these products and _____.

    d. Stars have a life cycle just like everything else in the universe. After a star is born, it _____ (which can be billions of years) giving off light and heat.

    e. There are many books today on exercise, healthy eating, and fashion. They are designed to _____, but I just need my family and friends to be happy.

2 Underline the word which does NOT collocate with the word in bold.

a.	**time:**	make it in	volunteer	food	be on
b.	**money:**	raise	show	make	donate
c.	**life:**	morning	save his	want a better	real
d.	**married:**	happily	angrily	recently	get

3 Complete the sentences using any of the word chunks from pages 90 and 91.

a. The students need to _____ for their trip.

b. I only had ten minutes to get to my interview, and I thought I would be late. Luckily, I was able to get a taxi and I _____ .

c. My parents have been together for over 40 years and they never fight. They have a lot of fun together. I think they are a very _____ couple.

d. My best friend was a life guard working on the beach in Florida last summer. On her last day at work she heard a man shouting for help. My friend swam out into the ocean and brought the man back to shore. Apparently, the man was very rich and bought my friend a car because she _____ .

e. A lot of people emigrate to the United States from countries like Puerto Rico, the Dominican Republic and Mexico because they _____ . However, some do not find it.

f. A lot of my friends will _____ to charities, such as OXFAM, the Salvation Army, and the Red Cross, but they will not give money to people begging in the street.

g. Our parents' generation got married in their 20s. These days many people are waiting until their 30s to _____ .

h. I like to help people, so every summer I like to _____ my _____ to a local charity and teach immigrants to read and write in English.

10

Urban Legends

Warm Up

1 What is an urban legend? Read the text to find out.

An urban legend is like a modern folktale. It may be true, but usually it isn't true or we cannot confirm if the story is true. Urban Legends are often sent by email as something that happened to a "friend of a friend."

2 Look at the three urban legends. One is true and two are false. Which urban legend do you think is true?

a. Using a cell phone at the gas station can cause explosions.

b. There is a personal computer the size of a pen.

c. A woman tried to dry her wet cat in her microwave oven.

3 How many urban legends do you know? Tell a partner your favorite one.

Reading Strategy: Visualizing

Most people see pictures (images) in their mind when reading in their first language. This is called **visualization**.

Readers will often see images of actions, people, and places. For example, when reading a newspaper article about education, readers may see their old school, teachers, and classrooms.

Visualizing helps the reader understand the text and remember it more effectively. If you can see what you are reading about, this demonstrates understanding. Visualizing also helps you deduce the meaning of words from context more easily, as well as helping you to make inferences, interpretations, and judgments.

Studies have shown that about 90 percent of people visualize when they read in their first language.

Strategy in Focus

1 **Read the story carefully, and decide what you think about this urban legend.**

a. It is true.   **b.** It never happened.   **c.** It is possible.   **d.** It is impossible.

A Class Psychology Experiment

A class of psychology students decided to carry out an experiment on their professor. They paid attention to the professor's lectures only when he was standing near a waste paper basket. Whenever the professor walked away from the waste paper basket, the students stopped listening to him and started talking. Eventually the professor was "trained" to stand next to the waste paper basket for the whole lecture.

The students then started turning the waste paper basket upside-down before every class. They trained the professor to lecture first with one foot on the waste paper basket, and then stand with both feet on the wastebasket. The experiment worked so well that the professor eventually began giving his lectures while standing on the waste paper basket.

2 **Circle the images you visualized in your mind while reading the story. Then tell a partner about any other images you visualized in your mind.**

a professor   students   a wastepaper basket   a classroom

students listening   students talking   a student moving the wastebasket

a professor standing on a wastepaper basket

Feedback:

While reading this urban legend, it is common to see the professor and the students in the classroom. You will have had your own images—they are probably different from the other students in your class. You may have seen images from your own life, when you were younger or now. You may also have remembered the smells and noises from classrooms you are familiar with.

The Billion-Dollar Giveaway

Before Reading

1 Have you ever received these kinds of emails?

a. An email saying you can earn money quickly and easily.

b. An email warning you about a computer virus.

c. An email asking you to forward the message to all your friends.

2 What do you do when you receive the emails described above?

a. Immediately delete them.

b. Read them and forward them to friends.

c. Read them and decide if you should reply.

While Reading

3 Read the email up to the end of the second paragraph. What is the main message?

a. It is telling you how to make money quickly and easily.

b. It is asking you to forward the message to your friends.

c. It is warning you about a computer virus.

4 Read the rest of the email and decide what you would do.

a. Delete it.   b. Reply to it.   c. Forward to it to your friends.

After Reading

5 Circle the images you visualized in your mind. Tell a partner if you visualized other images in your mind.

Nina Sandborn	Steve Gilburn	a computer firm's logo/icon	a computer product
money	a check	a newspaper	friends reading the email

6 Decide if the statements are probably true (**T**) or false (**F**).

a. **T**   **F**   This email from SLM Micron is spam.

b. **T**   **F**   For the next two weeks, SLM Micron will give you $245 every time you send the message to a friend.

c. **T**   **F**   SLM Micron will also give $200 every time your friend forwards the message.

d. **T**   **F**   Nina Sandborn has received $24,800 from SLM Micron for forwarding this message.

The Billion-Dollar Giveaway

PLEASE READ!!!! It was in the LA DAILY—It was in the news!!! To all of my friends, I do not usually forward messages, but this is from my good friend Nina Sandborn and she really is a lawyer. If she says that this will work—it will work.

Dear Friends: This is not spam. U.S. billionaire Steve Gilburn is sharing his fortune. SLM Micron is now one of the largest Internet companies in the world. To make sure that OpenWebX remains the most widely used program, SLM Micron is running a test.

When you send this email to friends, SLM Micron will track it for two weeks, and pay you for sending it. For every person that you send this email to, SLM Micron will pay you $245.00. For every person that you sent it to who forwards it on, SLM Micron will pay you an additional $200.00. Within two weeks, SLM Micron will contact you for your address and then send you a check.

I thought this was a scam, but two weeks after receiving this email and forwarding it on, SLM Micron contacted me for my address. Within days, I received a check for $24,800.

Please forward this to as many people as possible. My brother's girlfriend did this a few months ago. When I went to visit her, she showed me her check. It was for $4,300.

Word Work

7 **Complete these sentences with a word chunk from the text without looking at the text.**

a. I received a very funny email today about a man who tried to steal a car. I'll _____ **the message** to you so you can read it.

b. You have to be careful who you _____ **this email** to because some people may not like this type of joke.

c. Please invite _____ **as possible** to the party on Saturday night. The more people at the party the more fun it will be.

d. "Dad, I've run out of money. I can't pay my rent." "Don't worry, son. I'll _____ **check** right away."

Before Reading

1 The article *The One Penny College Fund* is about a college student who needed money. What do you think about when you think of college? Write down words you think could appear in the text.

graduation _____ _____ _____

tuition _____ _____ _____

classes _____ _____ _____

While Reading

2 As you read the text, try to visualize images in your mind.

After Reading

3 Circle the images you visualized in your mind. Tell a partner if you visualized other images in your mind.

a college campus	a newspaper	someone sending money
books	college classes	people reading newspapers
college students	a journalist	someone writing a check

4 Tell a partner what you think of this urban legend.
  a. It is true. This could happen.
  b. It is not true. No one would send one penny to a student.
  c. I am not sure if it is true. It could happen but it seems like a strange story.

5 Check [✓] the inferences you can make about the text.
  a. _____ Mike Hayes only needed one cent to pay his tuition fees and college expenses.
  b. _____ The Chicago Tribune newspaper agreed to help Hayes because it was a good story.
  c. _____ Hayes thought his idea would be successful because everyone can give one penny.
  d. _____ Hayes was the best student in his class.

6 Underline the words, phrases, or sentences that support your inferences in activity 5.

The One Penny College Fund

Mike Hayes of Rochelle, Illinois, proved he was smart in his first year at college. In 1987, while he was a freshman at the University of Illinois, he came up with an idea to solve his tuition fee [5] and college expenses problem. Hayes thought everyone could spare a penny.

He wrote to Chicago Tribune writer Bob Greene with a request. Hayes wanted each of the newspaper's readers to send him a penny. [10] Greene thought the idea sounded fun and agreed to do it.

"Just one penny," Hayes said. "A penny doesn't mean anything to anyone. If everyone who is reading your column looks around the room right [15] now, there will be a penny under a cushion, or on the corner of the desk, or on the floor. That's all I'm asking. A penny from each of your readers."

In less than a month, the Many Pennies for Mike [20] fund had around 2.3 million pennies. Not everyone sent merely a penny—many sent nickels, dimes, quarters, and even more. Donations were received from every state in the United States, plus Mexico, Canada, and the [25] Bahamas. So, Hayes reached his $28,000 target and went on to earn his degree in food science from the University of Illinois.

Perhaps the last word is best left to his father, Bill Hayes: "When Mike first told me about his [30] idea, I just laughed and said that I thought it was dumb—which shows you that he's smarter than I am."

Word Work

7 Use these word chunks to write sentences about Mike Hayes without looking at the text.

a. first year at college: _____

b. he came up with an idea to: _____

c. donations were received: _____

d. reached his target: _____

Before Reading

1 Look at the pictures below. Tell a partner who you would help if you saw them hitchhiking and why.

2 Read the first two sentences of the story. What do you think the story will be about?

A young woman was driving back home from a party late one rainy night. She had been driving for 20 minutes on a country road when she saw a gray-haired woman by the side of the road.

a. _____ Tips for hitchhiking.

b. _____ Why people should not give rides to strangers.

c. _____ A scary story about an old woman.

While Reading

3 As you read the story, try to visualize images in your mind, and decide if this urban legend is true.

After Reading

4 Check [✓] any of these images you visualized in your mind while reading the story. Describe these images and any other images you visualized to a partner.

a. _____ A young woman driving on a small dark road.

b. _____ An old woman talking to the driver through an open window.

c. _____ The old woman sitting in the back of a dark car.

d. _____ A hairy arm with a tattoo.

5 What do you think of this urban legend?

a. It is true. This could happen.

b. It is not true. I don't believe this happened.

c. I have heard this story before, so it could be true.

d. I have heard this story before, but it is not true.

The Hairy Hitchhiker

A young woman was driving back home from a party late one rainy night. She had been driving for 20 minutes on a country road when she saw a gray-haired woman by the side of the road. [5] Usually, Mary never picked up hitchhikers, but it was a cold night and it was an old woman, so she stopped her car. Mary asked the old woman if she needed a ride. The old woman nodded and got in.

[10] "Do you live near here?" Mary asked.

"No," answered the passenger, in a soft voice, "I'm just going to visit a friend. He was going to meet me, but his car won't start, so I decided to hitchhike. There isn't a bus at this time, but [15] I knew someone would give me a ride."

Something in the way the old lady spoke made Mary uneasy about this strange hitchhiker. She didn't know why, but Mary felt that there was something wrong, something dangerous. But [20] how could an old lady be dangerous?

The hitchhiker turned to give the young driver some candy. As she took the candy, Mary noticed the old woman's hands were very large, and had no wrinkles. She also saw thick hair [25] and a tattoo on the woman's left arm. This wasn't an old woman. It was a young man!

Mary was scared and didn't know what to do, but she quickly thought of a plan. She suddenly stopped the car and said she had hit something. [30] She asked the old woman to take a look. When the hitchhiker was out of the car, Mary drove off.

Thinking she had made a mistake, Mary felt guilty—the hitchhiker was surely not a young [35] man meaning she had left an old woman at the side of a road far from any houses. She felt even worse when she noticed she still had the old woman's bag in her car. She opened the bag to look for information about the hitchhiker's [40] identity and saw that it was filled with wallets, jewelry, and a large, bloody knife.

Word Work

6 **Rewrite the word chunks to correct the mistakes.**

a. A young woman was **driving return home** from a party late one rainy night. _____

b. She asked the old woman if she **needed a drop off**. _____

c. The young woman was scared and **didn't know what to make**. _____

d. She asked the old lady to **take a watch**. _____

e. The young woman immediately **thought guilty**. _____

Reflection

▶ Which was your favorite text in this unit? Why?

▶ Which reading strategies did you use in this unit?

▶ Which new word chunks will you make an effort to use in the next five days? Choose at least five.

11

Relationship Myths

Warm Up

What is the relationship between the people in the pictures (e.g., friends, work colleagues etc.)? Write your idea under each picture.

A _____

B _____

C _____

Reading Strategy: Summarizing

While and after reading a text, it is often useful to **summarize** what you have read. You can do this in your mind, and you can also write a **summary**.

When you summarize a text, you identify the main ideas and other important details. It is not necessary to remember everything that you have read.

These questions will help you summarize a text:

- What is the text about?
- Who is the text about?
- What happens? When? Where?
- Why did the author write the text?

Now read the following news story and choose the best summary:

> James Blake knew something was wrong when he walked into the bank. Blake, the bank manager of New York Trust, noticed that the overnight security guard was missing. He then saw that the doors to the bank vault were open. When Blake went into the vault, he noticed that all the money was missing. Blake's bank was one of three banks in the city that was robbed last night.

a. There were three bank robberies in New York last night. The New York Trust was one of them.

b. James Blake, the bank manager of New York Trust, was very surprised that his bank was robbed. He noticed that the security guard and money were missing.

c. New York Trust was robbed last night. It was the third time this bank was robbed.

Feedback:

The best summary is a. as it provides the key ideas in the text. Answer b. gives too much detail and c. is inaccurate.

Strategy in Focus

1 As you read the article, underline the most important ideas.

Happily Ever After?

Sally Gregory is putting her seven-year-old daughter to bed. Gregory's daughter is begging for her mom to read her the fairy tale, *Cinderella*. Although Gregory loves reading to her child, she does not like the message contained in the popular fairy tale.

"This fairy tale portrays the stepmother as evil, stepsisters as cheats and liars, and a girl who is passively waiting for her prince to come. I don't want my daughter to think that she has to wait for one true love to find her. I want her to question all the messages contained in such stories." Gregory says.

She isn't the only person to feel this way. A group of like-minded people started the group, Fairy Tale Busters. Their aim is to "bust", or show the truth, in fairy tales like Cinderella and Snow White. Just like Gregory, they want parents and children to challenge the messages contained in these stories.

2 Now read the summaries and decide which one is the best.

a. The article *Happily Ever After?* is about children getting false ideas about relationships from fairy tales. The group, "Fairy Tale Busters," wants children to question the messages contained in these popular stories.

b. The article discusses the lessons children can learn from reading popular fairy tales. Sally Gregory believes girls should be passive and wait for their "prince" to rescue them from their problems.

c. Sally Gregory doesn't want to read *Cinderella* to her daughter. It is her daughter's favorite story but it contains negative messages about stepmothers and sisters. Other parents don't like this fairy tale so they have started a group called "Fairy Tale Busters." The group wants to show the world that the messages behind *Cinderella* and *Snow White* are negative.

Feedback:

The best summary is **a.** The main idea of the reading is that children learn unrealistic messages from fairy tales.

Summary **b.** is not a good summary because some of the information is not correct. The writer does not want girls to wait for their prince.

Summary **c.** is not a good summary because it contains too many unimportant details.

Reading **1** Dating Myths

Before Reading

1 Decide if you agree [✓] or disagree [×] with these statements. Then discuss your answers with a partner.

a. _____ Your boyfriend/girlfriend should be your best friend.

b. _____ You should never fight with your boyfriend/girlfriend.

c. _____ You should have the same interests as your partner.

d. _____ As long as you love each other, money is not important.

e. _____ If your partner has a bad habit, you can change it.

While Reading

2 As you read the text, underline the important ideas. For example, you may want to underline the ideas that tell you:

- What the text is about.
- Who the text is about.
- What the writer thinks.

After Reading

3 Choose the best ending to the summary.

The article describes some of the ideas people have about romantic relationships ...

a. It explains that couples in long-term relationships will eventually share the same interests and become very good friends. Often these couples become very similar and learn to change to make each other happy.

b. It explains that many couples say they are perfect for each other because they don't argue and they share the same interests. However, it is natural and healthy to argue if you still respect your partner.

c. It explains that sometimes it is healthy to argue with your partner, and that you don't have to share all your partner's interests. The article also explains that it is important to keep your friends and not to try to change your partner.

4 According to the text, are these statements true (**T**) or false (**F**)?

a. **T** **F** In a good relationship, a couple doesn't have to agree on everything.

b. **T** **F** In a perfect relationship, you share all the same interests as your partner.

c. **T** **F** It is important to maintain friendships with other people while dating.

d. **T** **F** Asking your partner to change something about himself/herself is OK if it will make you happier.

CD 2:
Track 14

Dating Myths

Many people have a certain idea about what makes a good relationship. Often it is connected to always getting along, being madly in love, and having the same interests, but many experts [5] say that relying on this idea is actually a recipe for disaster. These are common myths learned from fairy tales and popular movies. A healthy relationship is much more complex than what you see in the movies.

[10] **A healthy couple doesn't fight**

It is natural to have disagreements with your partner. The important thing is how you deal with your differences. Do you walk away or yell if you don't get your way, or do you listen to [15] what your partner has to say? It is healthy to fight as long as you respect the other person's ideas and feelings.

A good couple should be interested in the same things

[20] Although it is important to share some interests, don't change what you like to do just because your partner doesn't like the same thing. If you try to be something you are not, you may start to resent your partner.

[25] **Your partner should be your best friend**

Your partner is the person you spend the most time with, but should you be best friends? Maybe

not. Don't forget the person who was your best friend before you started dating. Who else can [30] you talk to about any problems you have in your relationship?

I'll be happy once my partner changes

This is one of the biggest relationship myths around. A partner is NOT a project. If you think, "I'd love him more if he were more ...," maybe [35] you need to reconsider your relationship.

Word Work

7 | Complete the sentences with these word chunks.

| walked away | don't get my way | deal with our differences | are madly in love |

a. I was so angry after the fight with my boyfriend that I _____.

b. My girlfriend and I _____ . When we're not together, we're always talking on the phone.

c. I get angry when my parents don't let me go out dancing or watch late-night TV. I hate it when I

_____ .

d. My best friend and I _____ in different ways. I like to talk about them but he likes to ignore them and pretend they don't exist.

Before Reading

1 **Decide how to summarize a text. Choose the statements you think are correct.**

When summarizing a text, try to remember:
a. The important ideas.
b. Some of the important details.
c. All the facts mentioned in the text.
d. All the numbers and names in the text.
e. What the text is about, who the text is about and what happened.

2 **You are going to read an article about a young man and a young woman. Look at the title. What do you think the article is about?**
a. The benefits and problems of friendship between males and females.
b. A story about two people who were not friends.
c. How to make friends.

3 **Read the first paragraph and decide if you want to change your hypothesis.**

While Reading

4 **As you read, think about the following questions.**
a. Who is the text about?
b. What is the text about?
c. Why is this included in the Relationship Myths unit?

After Reading

5 **Ask your partner about the article.**

Do you agree with the author that young men and women can be friends? Why or why not?

6 **Read the summaries and decide which one is the best.**
a. The article is about Sarah and Dan who are best friends. They play soccer together and go to the movies together. Everyone thinks they are dating each other but they are just friends.
b. The article asks if boys and girls can be friends without romantic feelings for each other. Through Dan and Sarah, the article explains the benefits of male–female friendships, and that male–female friendships are possible.
c. The author talks about why boys and girls should be friends with each other. The article explains how Sarah and Dan find it difficult to be friends because everyone thinks they should be dating.

CD 2:
Track 15

Just Friends?

Sarah and Dan often spend their weekends hanging out together; going to movies, shopping, or talking in a coffee shop. Many people, including their parents, think that they are more than just [5] friends but Sarah and Dan both disagree. "Why can't we just be friends and nothing more?" Sarah asks. Dan adds, "Most people see a boy and girl hanging out and automatically think they're dating, but we're just best friends who happen to be a [10] boy and a girl."

Can two people of the opposite sex just be best friends? Many people say that male–female friendships are simply a myth. They believe that romantic feelings will always make the friendship [15] difficult. Others believe that these kinds of friendships become a problem when the friends start dating other people. Jealousy becomes an issue and will hurt the friendship. However, people like Sarah and Dan argue that a friend is a friend, [20] gender is not the issue.

They also believe that such friendships have many benefits. The main one is that this kind of friendship allows you to see things from a different perspective. Young men often say that they can talk more openly [25] about their feelings with their female friends. They also say that being friends with a woman helps them to overcome their shyness about dating and makes them more confident. Young women mention that their male friends help them understand what [30] men are really thinking.

Sarah and Dan agree that the benefits outweigh any problems that their friendship has, such as people thinking that they are dating. As Sarah says, "It's the 21st Century, so why can't men [35] and women just be friends?"

Word Work

7 Circle your answers to these questions.

  a. Do you have friends of **the opposite sex**? Yes, I do / No, I don't.
  b. Can you **talk openly** about your feelings with your father? Yes, I can. / No, I can't.
  c. Would you like to know **what** your friends **are really thinking**? Yes, I would. / No, I wouldn't.
  d. Do you agree that having a close friendship with someone of the opposite gender would **make you more confident**?   Yes, I do / No, I don't.

Before Reading

1 Check [✓] the statements you agree with in the "Me" column.

	Me	Jason	Hannah
a. Parents don't want their children to grow up.	☐	☐	☐
b. Parents want their children to help out at home.	☐	☐	☐
c. Parents want to control their teenage children's lives.	☐	☐	☐
d. Parents don't trust their children's decisions.	☐	☐	☐

While Reading

2 Jason Jones is writing to Hannah, an agony aunt, for advice about his relationship with his parents. As you read the text, decide if you agree with Hannah's advice to Jason.

After Reading

3 Check [✓] the statements in the chart above that Jason and Hannah agree with.

4 Ask a partner questions about the text.
   a. Do you share Jason's feelings towards your own parents?
   b. Do you agree with Hannah's advice?

5 Choose three sentences that best complete a summary of the texts.

Jason is a teenage boy who is writing to a newspaper for advice about his relationship with his parents ...
   a. He feels his parents make too many decisions for him and he wants to be treated more like an adult.
   b. His parents treat him like a ten-year-old child, by asking him where he is going and what he is doing.
   c. Jason doesn't want to take care of his younger brother.
   d. Hannah explains that his feelings about his parents are common in teenagers.
   e. She thinks Jason may have gotten into trouble, so his parents should ask him lots of questions.
   f. She says that his parents will treat him like an adult if he acts like an adult.

CD 2:
Track 16

Teenagers and Their Parents

Dear Hannah,

I'm a 16-year-old boy and I have always gotten along with my parents. I thought that as I got older, my parents would start treating me more [5] like an adult, but they don't. Even though I'm a good student and don't get into trouble, they treat me like I am ten. They are always asking where I'm going, what I'm doing, who I'm hanging out with. It's like they don't trust me. [10] They are trying to control my life and have no idea what it's like to be a teenager. My parents don't care about what I want—they only care about what I do for them, like taking care of my younger brother. Although I love my parents, [15] they are driving me crazy. How can I show them that I am a mature adult?

Yours,

Jason

Dear Jason,

[20] The teenage years, when children are becoming adults, are often filled with parent-teenager misunderstandings. Although it is a time of great changes, it doesn't have to result in family conflict.

[25] Many teenagers feel the same way you do, that their parents are controlling, don't understand them, and don't want them to have fun. Those are common feelings that often result in misunderstandings. Your parents want you to [30] enjoy life but they don't want you to get hurt. You may have gotten into trouble before, which made your parents worry about you. Ask yourself, "Will they treat me more like an adult if I act like one?"

[35] Another common myth is that parents don't understand what it is like to be a teenager. Perhaps they don't understand because you are not talking to them. Remember, they were teenagers once and will probably have some good advice if you [40] take the time to talk and to listen.

You also mentioned that your parents ask you to help at home. It is only natural that you should help with household responsibilities if you are living with your parents. It is one way to learn [45] what it feels like to be an adult. Are you really doing as much as you can to help and do you help without being asked?

Yours,

Hannah

Word Work

6 Match the word chunk with its definition. Then choose one word chunk and write a sentence about yourself or someone you know.

a. get along with   •   •   **i.** annoy

b. drive someone crazy   •   •   **ii.** look after

c. get into trouble   •   •   **iii.** have a good relationship

d. take care of   •   •   **iv.** do something wrong

Reflection

▶ Which was your favorite text in this unit? Why?

▶ Which reading strategies did you use in this unit?

▶ Which new word chunks will you make an effort to use in the next five days? Choose at least five.

Warm Up

What is the best way to have an adventure? Rank these different adventures from 1 (the best way for you) to 4 (the worst way for you).

Reading Strategy: Planning your reading

To read effectively, you must understand the task—the reason why you are reading. Are you reading:

- to take a multiple choice test?
- for pleasure and interest?
- to take part in a discussion?
- to write an essay?

It is important to **know why you are reading** something. Then you can plan how carefully you need to read it, and plan how much time you want to spend reading.

For example, you are going to read a best-selling novel **for pleasure**. How are you going to read it? Do you skim the text for the main ideas? Or, do you scan the text for key details? You would probably read the whole text quickly and not too carefully.

In a **multiple choice test**, for example, you would read the question first and scan the text looking for key words, facts, names, or dates to give you the answer.

If you are using the text to give you ideas **for a discussion**, you don't need to understand the whole text, so you could skim the text looking for its main ideas. This will give you ideas for your discussion, but you don't have to spend time trying to understand everything and all the details. You only need to contribute to the discussion with what you understand and agree with.

When you are preparing **to write an essay**, you usually read a text carefully so you understand its ideas well and how the ideas are supported. You may want to include the ideas in your essay with your own examples, adding your own thoughts.

Strategy in Focus

1 You are reading the following article because you think it may be interesting. Decide how to read the story.

a. _____ Scan for key words and facts.　　**b.** _____ Skim for the main ideas.

c. _____ Read everything carefully.　　**d.** _____ Read everything one time quickly.

2 Read the story and tell a partner if you think it is interesting.

Rover's Great Adventure

Rover, a Golden Retriever dog, survived a 160-foot fall down a cliff in southern California yesterday. After tumbling down the cliff, Rover landed next to the busy Pacific Coast Highway and just missed being hit by a truck.

A motorist who was parked nearby and had witnessed the events whistled for Rover, who jumped straight into her car. The rescuer says that as soon as Rover got into the car, he started licking her face.

But Rover's owner did not know about the rescue. Karl Robinson lost sight of Rover when the dog started to chase a wild rabbit. Robinson ran to the cliff and started looking for his dog. Robinson ended up getting stuck himself as he attempted to climb down the cliff to find Rover and he had to call for help using his cell phone.

Robinson was eventually rescued by firefighters and he was quickly reunited with Rover.

3 You are going to answer a multiple choice question about the news story. Decide how you will read the text this time.

a. Read everything one time quickly.　　**b.** Read everything carefully.

c. Skim for the main ideas.　　**d.** Scan for key words and facts.

4 Answer this multiple choice question about the text.

Robinson is the:

a. Name of the dog.　　**b.** The dog's owner.

c. The women who rescued the dog.　　**d.** The firefighter who rescued the dog.

Feedback:

The answers are 1 a., 3 d., and 4 b.

Have a Real Adventure

Before Reading

1 You are going to read an article to give you ideas for a discussion. Decide how you will read the article. Choose the best strategy for the task.

Discussion Topic: The best way to travel and have an adventure

a. _____ Scan for key words and facts.   **b.** _____ Skim for the main ideas.

c. _____ Read everything carefully.   **d.** _____ Read everything one time quickly.

2 Which modes of transportation are best for an adventure?

a. _____ airplane   **b.** _____ hitchhiking   **c.** _____ train   **d.** _____ ship

e. _____ motorcycle   **f.** _____ car   **g.** _____ bus   **h.** _____ bicycle

While Reading

3 Read the article quickly and without stopping. While reading, circle the types of transportation the writer mentions.

After Reading

4 Discuss your answer to activity 2 with a partner. Why did you choose those modes of transportation?

a. It is exciting.

b. You can meet local people.

c. It is quick and comfortable.

d. You see more of the country.

e. You can make your own travel schedule.

f. Your idea: _____

5 Choose the best ending to the summary.

The article explains that some people travel overland rather than on airplanes so they can have a better experience of a country ...

a. It describes how the Sanders drove their motorcycle to South America. It took them 35 days and they traveled 20,000 miles. They also traveled around the world on their motorcycle in 19 days.

b. It describes how some people travel on motorbikes, by train, and by hitch-hiking all over the world to have more of an adventure. People traveling this way say they have more freedom and meet more people.

Have a Real Adventure

Airplanes are the preferred mode of transportation for many people when taking a long trip. For others, cruise ships offer the best option. Yet, some travelers scorn these modes of popular [5] transportation. For them, the only way to truly experience a country is traveling overland by motorcycle, train, or hitchhiking.

Kevin and Julia Sanders are two well-known overland travelers. In 35 days they rode by [10] motorcycle from Alaska to the tip of South America, a journey of 20,000 miles (32,000 km) across 14 countries. The Sanders also traveled around the world by motorcycle in just over 19 days. Kevin believes that traveling by bike gives [15] people more freedom because you never have to worry about bus or train schedules. Instead, you can organize your time the way you want.

If you prefer to travel in a little more comfort, trains are another popular overland option. The [20] train gives travelers the opportunity to interact with locals, and to go off the beaten track. Exploring western Europe by train is a very popular adventure for college students as the train system is excellent, affordable, and easy [25] to navigate.

For the truly adventurous, hitchhiking can be an exciting way to see a country. Hitching can be quite dangerous and is not recommended in many countries, but when it is safe enough to do so, [30] travelers love it. It is a guaranteed way to meet people, and hitchhikers often learn things not found in travel guides.

Word Work

6 Find a word chunk from the article with the same meaning as these phrases. Write the word chunk next to the phrase. Then write a sentence using one word chunk.

a. Favorite way to travel: _____

b. To really understand a county's culture: _____

c. To go to places other tourists don't visit: _____

My Australian Adventure

Before Reading

1 Your teacher suggests that you read *My Australian Adventure* because you may enjoy it. After you read the story, your teacher will also ask you to talk about a trip you have taken. Decide how you will read the article.

a. _____ Scan for key words and facts. b. _____ Skim for the main ideas.

c. _____ Read everything carefully. d. _____ Read everything one time quickly.

2 Make a list of words/things you associate with Australia.

_____ _____ _____ _____

_____ _____ _____ _____

While Reading

3 While you read the story, try to visualize images in your mind.

After Reading

4 Describe the clearest image you visualized to a partner.

5 Tell your partner if you found the story:

a. interesting b. amusing c. boring d. silly

6 Tell your partner about a trip you have taken, answering these questions:

Where did you go? When did you go? How long did you go for?

Who did you go with? What did you do? Did you have a good time?

7 Read the story again. Check [✓] the inferences you can make.

a. _____ The conference was in Brisbane.

b. _____ Chris hit a kangaroo when he was driving too quickly.

c. _____ Chris thought the kangaroo was dead.

d. _____ Chris saved the kangaroo's life.

e. _____ Chris and the writer found the kangaroo, and got the jacket back.

f. _____ Chris and the writer didn't have extra car keys.

My Australian Adventure

A couple of years ago, I went to Australia for a conference with my colleague, Chris. We decided to drive across country to Brisbane after the conference ended. The drive was going to take [5] four days and most of it was across the desert, so we had to take food, water, and extra gas with us.

The first day was a lot of fun as we were excited and laughing at each other's stupid jokes. By the [10] third day of driving in the seemingly endless desert, we began to get bored. We had been quiet for a few hours when in the distance Chris spotted some kangaroos. We were both excited and decided to get a closer look. Chris accelerated to catch up [15] with the kangaroos. We got closer and closer, and Chris was doing 110 kilometers per hour. We were very close to the kangaroos—too close—when we heard a loud BANG!

Chris stopped the car and we got out. Behind [20] the car was a large kangaroo lying completely still on the ground. Chris went over to the kangaroo and put his baseball cap on its head. He took off his sunglasses and put them on the kangaroo and did the same with his jacket. Then, [25] he put his arm around the kangaroo and told me to take a photo of them together. I was still in shock, but I took out my camera. While I was focusing the camera, I saw the kangaroo move. It suddenly woke up, looked at Chris, and hopped [30] away into the distance before we could do anything.

I started laughing but Chris looked very serious. He said his wallet and passport were in the jacket. I started laughing even harder. I stopped [35] laughing, however, when he said that our car keys were also in the jacket!

Word Work

8 **Rewrite the word chunks to correct the mistakes.**

a. We have a long drive tomorrow. I want to be **in a road** by 8:00 a.m. _____

b. There was a large crowd gathering on the other side of the street, so I crossed the road to **take a nearer look**. They were watching some young kids dancing. _____

c. **A few of years ago** I went camping with my friends. We had a great time. _____

d. I want to go to China one day, so I can **give a photo** standing on the Great Wall. _____

e. Whenever I am feeling sad, my mom **takes her arm over** me to help me feel better. _____

Before Reading

1 You are going to read an article about Hendrick Hamel for a short multiple choice test. Decide how you will read the article. You only have two minutes to take the test.

a. _____ Scan for key words and facts.   **b.** _____ Skim for the main ideas.

c. _____ Read everything carefully.   **d.** _____ Read everything one time quickly.

While Reading

2 Look at the questions below and scan the text for the answers.

After Reading

3 Complete the sentences to answer the multiple choice questions.

a. From the 1400s to the 1800s European explorers:
  - **i.** were paid to find countries to trade with and colonize.
  - **ii.** became very rich in Africa, South America, and Africa.
  - **iii.** couldn't travel to Asian countries.

b. According to the text, Hendrick Hamel:
  - **i.** was sent to Korea on a trading mission.
  - **ii.** was a sailor and explorer from the Netherlands.
  - **iii.** was in a shipping accident returning from Japan.

c. Korea:
  - **i.** was colonized by the Dutch in the 16th Century.
  - **ii.** was not trading with the rest of the world in the early 17th century.
  - **iv.** had its capital on Jeju Island in the 17th century.

d. Hendrick Hamel:
  - **i.** spent 13 years writing about Korea and its people.
  - **ii.** was given permission to write about Korea by its government.
  - **iii.** spent 13 years in a Korean prison.

Hendrick Hamel's Korean Adventure

From the 15th to 19th centuries, many European countries paid explorers and companies to create trade routes and discover new countries around the world. This resulted in Europe colonizing
[5] many African, South American, and Asian countries. In the Netherlands, the Dutch East India Company was the major company to run these trade routes. They paid people to sail to countries in South America and Asia.

[10] Hendrick Hamel was a bookkeeper for the Dutch East India Company. He was sent on a trading mission to Japan in 1653. On the trip back, he was shipwrecked on an island near Korea. Of the 64 sailors, only 36 survived the accident.

[15] In the early 17th Century, Korea was a "closed" country. It had seen the effects of colonization and wanted to protect itself from outside influence. As a result, they did not welcome foreigners into their country and Korea was therefore unknown
[20] to the rest of the world. There was no published information on the country, the people, or their customs available in Europe at that time.

When Hamel's ship crashed on Jeju Island, the Korean government rescued the sailors and
[25] brought them to the capital, Seoul. Although the sailors were given some freedom within Korea, they could not go home. Foreigners were not allowed to leave the country because the government feared they would tell others about
[30] Korea. For 13 years, Hamel and his shipmates lived among the Koreans. Hamel wrote about the country and its customs in his journals.

After 13 years, Hamel and seven of his shipmates managed to escape from Korea to Japan, where
[35] they found a boat going back to the Netherlands. On his return home, Hamel's writings on Korea were published. This was the first information Europeans had about Korea.

Word Work

4 **Complete the word chunks in the sentences below with words from the box.**

this often resulted in	on the trip back from	the rest of the world
wrote about	in her journal	

a. During the Second World War, Anne Frank hid with her family. She _____ her experiences _____. She became internationally famous when her journal was published in 1947.

b. Football and baseball are national sports in America, but in _____ other sports are more popular.

c. Mick always left his homework until the last minute. _____ him needing to stay up all night to finish the work.

d. Last year, we flew to Shanghai from Beijing in China. We didn't see much of the country or people, so _____ Beijing we took the train.

Reflection

▶ Which was your favorite text in this unit? Why?

▶ Which reading strategies did you use in this unit?

▶ Which new word chunks will you make an effort to use in the next five days? Choose at least five.

Review Reading Strategies

- Unit 10: Visualizing
- Unit 11: Summarizing
- Unit 12: Planning your reading

1 Which reading strategies do these sentences describe? Read each statement and check [✓] the best answer.

		Visualizing	Summarizing	Planning Your Reading
a.	Think about the reason why you are reading the text.			
b.	Think about who and what the text is about.			
c.	See images in your mind of people in the text.			
d.	Decide if you are reading the text for pleasure or a test.			
e.	See pictures in your mind of places in the text.			
f.	Think about what happens in the text.			
g.	Remember the main ideas of the text.			
h.	See images of places, people, and events from your own life which are similar to the text.			
i.	See images in your mind of the events in the text.			
j.	Think about what you need to do.			

2 You are going to read a student's essay for a class discussion. Decide how to read the text.

a. _____ Scan for key words and facts.   b. _____ Skim for the main ideas.

c. _____ Read everything carefully.   d. _____ Read everything one time quickly.

3 As you read the text, try to visualize images. After you have read the text, tell a partner about the images you saw.

4 In groups, discuss if corporal punishment in schools should be legal.

5 Choose the best ending to the summary.

In the article, the writer thinks physical punishment is a bad idea ...

a. She says that although many American states allow corporal punishment in schools, it can cause psychological damage to the students, encourage them to be violent as adults, and cause physical harm.

b. She says that 300,000 schools in America discipline students with corporal punishment. They allow teachers to hit, beat and paddle students. She also says that students should be punished each day in these schools.

Reading

CD 2:
Track 20

Student : Marta Sanchez
Professor : Linda Lane
Date : August 13, 2008

Corporal Punishment in U.S. Schools

[1] Parents send their children to school to be educated and learn how to behave in the community. Most parents assume that school is a safe environment yet they may not know that when their children get into trouble they could be physically harmed. Many U.S. schools still use corporal punishment, such as hitting, beating, or paddling for disciplinary purposes.

[2] According to federal statistics, over 300,000 American school children were disciplined with corporal punishment in the year 2002–3, and 22 states still allow it to be used in schools, including Texas and Louisiana. I think that corporal punishment should be stopped. Hitting has physical effects on students and may also cause psychological damage. Adults are responsible for taking care of children, not harming them.

[3] One reason why we should stop corporal punishment in our schools is that this method has harmful psychological effects on children. Many children may lie and not take responsibility for their bad behavior because they are afraid of the punishment. Moreover, punishing children this way can lead to further violence. Studies have found that children who were hit often turned into adults who do not get along with others and used violence against their own loved ones.

[4] When corporal punishment is allowed in schools, it becomes easier for some adults to hurt children. There are many reports of students who have been severely beaten in schools that allow corporal punishment. When parents realize that their own children may be physically harmed, they are often against the idea of using corporal punishment as a method of discipline. Although they want their children to behave in school, they don't want them to be hurt.

[5] The best way of dealing with children's misbehavior is by preventing it. Parents and teachers should work together to encourage children to be responsible and respectful in the classroom. Adults and children should talk openly and deal with their differences in a non-violent way. If punishment is needed, volunteer service in the school, detention, or even suspension can be arranged. As Dr. Robert E. Fathman, President of the National Coalition to Abolish Corporal Punishment in Schools said, "Good school discipline should be instilled through the mind, not the behind."

Comprehension Check

1 It can be inferred that the writer of this essay:

    a. believes that corporal punishment should be used in some schools.

    b. disagrees with the use of hitting as a disciplinary method in school.

    c. believes that parents should discipline their children at home.

    d. is against using punishment in American schools.

2 The writer probably mentions the fact that over 300,000 schoolchildren were disciplined with corporal punishment to show that ...

    a. it is still widely used as a form of punishment in schools in the USA.

    b. Students in the USA do not take school seriously and are irresponsible.

    c. most students misbehave in schools in America.

    d. teachers have no control over students in their classrooms.

3 The word "corporal" in the passage is closest in meaning to:

    a. dangerous   **b.** harmful   **c.** painful   **d.** physical

4 In paragraph 4, the word "they" refers to:

    a. children and parents   **b.** children

    c. parents   **d.** teachers and students

5 Choose three sentences that best complete a summary of the text.

Corporal punishment is a disciplinary method used in some schools in the USA ...

    a. Corporal punishment may involve hitting, spanking, or paddling students.

    b. Robert Fathman is the director of a national organization against corporal punishment.

    c. Those who support it believe that it helps teach respect and good manners to students.

    d. Teachers should work with parents when deciding whether to use corporal punishment.

    e. Students who are punished usually become violent adults.

    f. Those who oppose it do so because of the physical and emotional effects it may have on students.

More Word Chunks

1 Complete the summary using these word chunks from Units 10, 11 and 12.

got along with	come up with an idea	as many people as possible
sent an email	take a trip abroad	forward the message
send me a check		

After I graduated from college, I wanted to **a.** _____, so I decided to spend three months backpacking around Europe. I thought I had saved enough money for the trip, but two months into my travel I realized I had no money. I needed to **b.** _____ to make some money. I didn't know what to do. I found an Internet cafe and **c.** _____ to all my friends and family asking for advice. I also asked them to **d.** _____ to **e.** _____. Although no one volunteered to **f.** _____, they did give me a lot of suggestions. One person suggested that I to go to the local university and advertise English conversation/culture classes. I followed that advice, put up an advertisement, and received a few calls on the first day. I started teaching and really loved it. I **g.** _____ the students, met some interesting people, and made enough money for the rest of my trip.

2 In Units 10 and 12 we learned about the word chunks "take a look" and "take a photo."

The young woman asked the old lady to take a look outside the car.
He told me to take a photo of them together.

Here are some other common word chunks with "take."

take a peek	take a break	take a moment
take a vacation	take a taxi	take a walk

In Unit 11 we learned about word chunks with "get."

get along with	get my way	get into trouble
get in the way	get older	

Here are some other common chunks with "get."

get around	get back (to)	get away	get together
get out	get up	get by	get over

Change the bold words in the sentence using a word chunk from this page.

a. I've been studying for my English test for two hours and I need to **stop for a while**.

_____

b. I usually take public transportation when I need to **go somewhere** in the city.

_____

c. Every Friday night, I enjoy **meeting up** with my friends and going to a cafe.

_____

d. I find it easy to **meet and talk with** everybody, no matter how old or young.

_____

			Page
accelerate	/æksɛləreɪt/	V-I When a moving vehicle accelerates, it goes faster and faster.	113
act	/ækt/	V-I If someone acts in a particular way, they behave in that way.	107
ad	/æd/	N-COUNT An advertisement. [INFORMAL]	69
adoption	/ədɒpʃən/	N-VAR Adoption involves taking someone else's child into your own family and make the child legally your own son or daughter.	47
advice column	/ædvaɪs kɒləm/	N-COUNT In a newspaper or magazine, the advice column contains letters from readers about their personal problems, and advice on what to do about them.	39
agricultural	/ægrɪkʌltʃərəl/	ADJ Agricultural means involving or relating to farming crops and animals.	49
argue	/ɑrgyu/	V-T If you argue that something is true, you state it and give the reasons why you think it is true.	105
arranged marriage	/əreɪndʒd mærɪdʒ/	N-COUNT In an arranged marriage, the parents choose the person who their son or daughter will marry.	67
assassinate	/əsæsɪneɪt/	V-T When someone important is assassinated, they are murdered as a political act.	85
athlete	/æθlit/	N-COUNT An athlete is a person who does any kind of physical sports, exercise, or games, especially in competitions.	19
attention	/ətɛnʃən/	N-UNCOUNT Attention is great interest that is shown in someone or something.	11
attitude	/ætɪtud/	N-VAR Your attitude to something is the way that you think and feel about it, especially when this shows in the way you behave.	83
automatically	/ɔtəmætɪkəli/	ADV If you do something automatically, you do it without thinking about it.	105
awake	/əweɪk/	ADJ Someone who is awake is not sleeping.	87
award	/əwɔrd/	N-COUNT An award is a prize or certificate that a person is given for doing something well.	83
beat	/bit/	V-T If you beat someone or something, you hit them very hard.	85
beg	/bɛg/	V-T/ V-I If you beg someone to do something, you ask them very anxiously or eagerly to do it.	15
billion	/bɪlyən/	NUM A billion is a thousand million.	47
biological	/baɪəlɒdʒɪkəl/	ADJ A child's biological parents are the man and woman who caused him or her to be born, rather than other adults who raise him or her.	47
blood pressure	/blʌd prɛʃər/	N-UNCOUNT Your blood pressure is the amount of force with which your blood flows around your body.	75
boarding school	/bɔrdiŋ skul/	N-VAR A boarding school is a school that some or all of the students live in during the school term.	59
bookkeeper	/bʊkkipər/	N-COUNT A bookkeeper is a person whose job is to keep an accurate record of the money that is spent and received by a business or other organization. [BUSINESS]	115
breathe	/brið/	V-T / V-I When people or animals breathe, they take air into their lungs and let it out again.	21
brick	/brɪk/	N-VAR Bricks are rectangular blocks of baked clay used for building walls, which are usually red or brown. Brick is the material made up of these blocks.	51
campaign	/kæmpeɪn	N-COUNT A campaign is a planned set of activities that people carry out over a period of time in order to achieve something such as social or political change.	77
carpet	/kɑrpɪt/	N-VAR A carpet is a thick covering of soft material which is laid over a floor or a staircase.	85
catch up with	/kætʃ ʌp wɪð/	PHRASAL VERB If you catch up with someone who is in front of you, you reach them by walking faster than they are walking.	113
celebrity	/sɪlɛbrɪti/	N-COUNT A celebrity is someone who is famous, especially in areas of entertainment such as movies, music, writing, or sports.	29

challenge	/ˈtʃælɪndʒ/	V-T If you challenge someone, you invite them to fight or compete with you in some way.	77
charity	/ˈtʃærɪti/	N-COUNT A charity is an organization which raises money in order to help people who are ill, disabled, or very poor.	55
client	/ˈklaɪənt/	N-COUNT A client of a professional person or organization is a person or company that receives a service from them in return for payment. [BUSINESS]	69
colleague	/ˈkɒlig/	N-COUNT Your colleagues are the people you work with, especially in a professional job.	113
colonize	/ˈkɒlənaɪz/	V-T If people colonize a foreign country, they go to live there and take control of it.	115
common	/ˈkɒmən/	ADJ If something is common, it is found in large numbers or it happens often.	67
community	/kəˈmyunɪti/	N-SING-COLL The community is all the people who live in a particular area or place.	49
company	/ˈkʌmpəni/	N-UNCOUNT Company is having another person or other people with you, usually when this is pleasant or stops you feeling lonely.	71
compare	/kəmˈpɛər/	V-T When you compare things, you consider them and discover the differences or similarities between them.	39
compete	/kəmˈpit/	V-RECIP If you compete with someone for something, you try to get it for yourself and stop the other person from getting it.	11
competitive	/kəmˈpɛtɪtɪv/	ADJ A competitive person is eager to be more successful than other people.	39
complain	/kəmˈpleɪn/	V-T/ V-I If you complain about a situation, you say that you are not satisfied with it.	43
computer programmer	/kəmˈpyutər proʊˈgræmər/	N-COUNT A computer programmer is a person whose job involves writing programs for computers. [COMPUTING]	41
conference	/ˈkɒnfərəns, -frəns/	N-COUNT A conference is a meeting, often lasting a few days, which is organized on a particular subject or to bring together people who have a common interest.	113
confidence	/ˈkɒnfɪdəns/	N-UNCOUNT If you have confidence, you feel sure about your abilities, qualities, or ideas.	19
confident	/ˈkɒnfɪdənt/	ADJ If a person or their manner is confident, they feel sure about their own abilities, qualities, or ideas.	27
confirm	/kənˈfɜrm/	V-T If something confirms what you believe, suspect, or fear, it shows that it is definitely true.	75
conflict	/ˈkɒnflɪkt/	N-UNCOUNT Conflict is serious disagreement and argument about something important.	107
construction	/kənˈstrʌkʃən/	N-UNCOUNT Construction is the building of things such as houses, factories, roads, and bridges.	49
controlling	/kənˈtroʊlɪŋ/	ADJ If you say that someone is controlling, you mean that they want to be in control of every situation they find themselves in.	107
courage	/ˈkɜrɪdʒ/	N-COUNT Courage is the quality shown by someone who decides to do something difficult or dangerous, even though they may be afraid.	83
crowd	/kraʊd/	N-COUNT-COLL A crowd is a large group of people who have gathered together, for example, to watch or listen to something interesting, or to protest against something.	59
custom	/ˈkʌstəm/	N-VAR A custom is an activity, a way of behaving, or an event which is usual or traditional in a particular society or in particular circumstances.	79
date	/deɪt/	V-RECIP If you are dating someone, you go out with them regularly because you are having, or may soon have, a romantic relationship with them. You can also say that two people are dating.	67
dating service	/ˈdeɪtɪŋ sɜrvɪs/	N-COUNT Dating agencies or services are for people who are trying to find a girlfriend or boyfriend.	69
dedicate	/ˈdɛdɪkeɪt/	V-T If someone dedicates something such as a book, play, or piece of music to you, they mention your name, for example, in the front of a book or when a piece of music is performed, as a way of showing affection or respect for you.	71
deed	/did/	N-COUNT A deed is something that is done, especially something that is very good or very bad. (LITERARY)	87

deforestation	/dɪfɔrɪsteɪʃən/	N-UNCOUNT Deforestation is the cutting down and destruction of all trees in an area.	79
demand	/dɪmænd/	V-T If you demand something such as information or action, you ask for it in a very forceful way.	43
depression	/dɪprɛʃən/	N-VAR Depression is a mental state in which you are sad and feel that you cannot enjoy anything, because your situation is so difficult and unpleasant.	19
determined	/dɪtɜrmɪnd/	ADJ If you are determined to do something, you have made a firm decision to do it and will not let anything stop you.	59
diamond	/daɪmənd/	N-VAR A diamond is a hard, bright, precious stone that is clear and colorless. Diamonds are used in jewelry and for cutting very hard substances.	87
direct	/dɪrɛkt, daɪ–/	ADV You use direct to describe an experience, activity, or system which only involves the people, actions, or things that are necessary to make it happen.	23
disadvantaged	/dɪsədvæntɪdʒd/	ADJ People who are disadvantaged or live in disadvantaged areas live in bad conditions and tend not to get a good education or have a reasonable standard of living.	49
disagreement	/dɪsəgrimənt/	N-VAR When there is disagreement about something, people disagree or argue about what should be done.	103
disappointment	/dɪsəpɔɪntmənt/	N-UNCOUNT Disappointment is the state of feeling rather sad because something has not happened or because something is not as good as you had hoped.	19
disease	/dɪziz/	N-VAR A disease is an illness which affects people, animals, or plants, for example one which is caused by bacteria or infection.	75
distribute	/dɪstrɪbyut/	V-T If you distribute things, you hand them or deliver them to a number of people.	77
donate	/doʊneɪt/	V-T If you donate something to a charity or other organization, you give it to them.	55
dormitory	/dɔrmɪtɔri/	N-COUNT A dormitory is a building at a college or university where students live.	27
due	/du/	ADJ If something is due at a particular time, it is expected to happen, be done, or arrive at that time.	57
dumb	/dʌm/	ADJ If you call a person dumb, you mean that they are stupid or foolish. [INFORMAL]	97
embryo	/embriəʊ – embrioʊ/	N-COUNT An embryo is a human in the very early stages of development in the womb.	
empty-handed	/ɛmpti hændid/	ADJ If you come away from somewhere empty-handed, you have failed to get what you wanted.	43
encourage	/ɪnkɜrɪdʒ/	V-T If you encourage someone to do something, you try to persuade them to do it, for example, by telling them that it would be a pleasant thing to do, or by trying to make it easier for them to do it. You can also encourage an activity.	77
energize	/ɛnərdʒaɪz/	V-T To energize someone means to give them the enthusiasm and determination to do something.	77
environment	/ɪnvaɪrənmənt, –vaɪərn–/	N-SING The environment is the natural world of land, sea, air, plants, and animals.	79
(soil) erosion	/sɔɪl ɪroʊʒən/	N-UNCOUNT Erosion is the gradual destruction and removal of rock soil in a particular area by rivers, the sea, or the weather.	79
eventually	/ɪvɛntʃuəli/	ADV Eventually means at the end of a situation or process or as the final result of it.	23
expand	/ɪkspænd/	V-T/V-I If something expands or is expanded, it becomes larger.	49
expenses	/ɪkspɛnsɪs/	N-PLURAL Expenses are amounts of money that you spend while doing something in the course of your work, which will be paid back to you afterward. [BUSINESS]	97
expert	/ɛkspɜrt/	N-COUNT An expert is a person who is very skilled at doing something or who knows a lot about a particular subject.	103
explorer	/ɪksplɔrər/	N-COUNT An explorer is someone who travels to places about which very little is known, in order to discover what is there.	115
factory	/fæktəri, –tri/	N-COUNT A factory is a large building where machines are used to make large quantities of goods.	23

fee	/fi/	N-COUNT A fee is the amount of money that a person or organization is paid for a particular job or service that they provide.	69
feed	/fid/	V-I When an animal feeds, it eats or drinks something.	83
fiancé	/fianseɪ, fianseɪ/	N-COUNT A woman's fiance is the man to whom she is engaged to be married.	15
fire	/faɪər/	V-T If an employer fires you, they dismiss you from your job.	47
flu	/flu/	N-UNCOUNT Flu is an illness which is similar to a bad cold but more serious. It often makes you feel very weak and makes your muscles hurt.	27
fortune	/fɔrtʃən/	N-COUNT You can refer to a large sum of money as a fortune or a small fortune to emphasize how large it is.	95
forward	/fɔrwərd/	V-T If a letter or message is forwarded to someone, it is sent to the place where they are, after having been sent to a different place earlier.	95
freshman	/frɛʃmən/	N-COUNT In America, a freshman is a student who is in his or her first year at university or college.	97
fund	/fʌnd/	N-COUNT A fund is an amount of money that is collected or saved for a particular purpose.	97
garbage	/gɑrbɪdʒ/	N-UNCOUNT Garbage is waste material, especially waste from a kitchen. [mainly AM]	55
gender	/dʒɛndər/	N-VAR A person's gender is the fact that they are male or female.	105
give birth	/gɪv bɜrθ/	PHRASE When a woman gives birth, she produces a baby from her body.	57
giveaway	/gɪvəweɪ/	N-COUNT A giveaway is something that a company or organization gives to someone, usually in order to encourage people to buy a particular product.	95
glad	/glæd/	ADJ If you are glad about something, you are happy and pleased about it.	67
glance	/glæns/	V-I If you glance at something or someone, you look at them very quickly and then look away again immediately.	71
grab	/græb/	V-T If you grab something, you take it or pick it up suddenly and roughly.	83
grade	/greɪd/	N-COUNT Your grade in an examination or piece of written work is the mark you get, usually in the form of a letter or number, that indicates your level of achievement.	31
graduation	/grædʒueɪʃən/	N-COUNT A graduation is a special ceremony at a university, college, or school, at which degrees and diplomas are given to students who have successfully completed their studies.	31
grateful	/greɪtfəl/	ADJ If you are grateful for something that someone has given you or done for you, you have warm, friendly feelings toward them and wish to thank them.	31
greedy	/gridi/	ADJ If you describe someone as greedy, you mean that they want to have more of something such as food or money than is necessary or fair.	29
greet	/grit/	V-T When you greet someone, you say 'Hello' or shake hands with them.	23
guaranteed	/gærəntid/	ADJ If you say that something is guaranteed to happen, you mean that you are certain that it will happen.	111
guard	/gɑrd/	N-COUNT A guard is someone such as a soldier, police officer, or prison officer who is guarding a particular place or person.	51
guess	/gɛs/	PHRASE You say I guess to show that you are slightly uncertain or reluctant about what you are saying. [mainly AM, INFORMAL, VAGUENESS]	51
guest	/gɛst/	N-COUNT A guest is someone who is staying in a hotel.	29
guy	/gaɪ/	N-COUNT A guy is a man. [INFORMAL]	71
hairy	/hɛəri/	ADJ Someone or something that is hairy is covered with hair.	99
happen	/hæpən/	V-T If you happen to do something, you do it by chance. If it happens that something is the case, it occurs by chance.	105
heartbroken	/hɑrtbroʊkən/	ADJ Someone who is heartbroken is very sad and emotionally upset.	15
hitchhiker	/hɪtʃhaɪkər/	N-COUNT A hitchhiker is someone who travels by getting lifts from passing vehicles without paying.	99
homeless shelter	/hoʊmlɪs ʃɛltər/	N-COUNT A homeless shelter is a building where homeless people can sleep and get food.	55

hop	/hɒp/	V-I When birds and some small animals hop, they move along by jumping on both feet.	113
hope	/hoʊp/	N-UNCOUNT Hope is a feeling of desire and expectation that things will go well in the future.	19
household	/haʊshoʊld/	N-SING The household is your home and everything that is connected with taking care of it.	107
imagine	/ɪmædʒɪn/	V-T If you imagine something, you think about it and your mind forms a picture or idea of it.	51
implant	/ɪmplænt/	V-T To implant something into a person's body means to put it there, usually by means of a medical operation.	57
independent	/ɪndɪpɛndənt/	ADJ If someone is independent, they do not need help or money from anyone else.	11
inspire	/ɪnspaɪər/	V-T If something or someone inspires a particular book, work of art, or action, they are the source of the ideas in it or act as a model for it.	21
instant	/ɪnstənt/	N-SING If you say that something happens at a particular instant, you mean that it happens at exactly the time you have been referring to, and you are usually suggesting that it happens quickly or immediately.	47
interact	/ɪntərækt/	V-RECIP When people interact with each other or interact, they communicate as they work or spend time together.	111
internship	/ɪntɜrnʃɪp/	N-COUNT An internship is the position held by an advanced student or a recent graduate, especially in medicine, who is being given practical training under supervision. (AM)	41
in vitro fertilization	/ɪn vitroʊ fɜrtəlɪzeɪʃən/	In vitro fertilization is a method of helping a woman to have a baby in which an egg is removed from one of her ovaries, fertilized outside her body, and then replaced in her womb.	57
janitor	/dʒænɪtər/	N-COUNT A janitor is a person whose job is to take care of a building. [mainly AM]	55
keep a straight face	/kip ə streɪt feɪs/	PHRASE If you manage to keep a straight face, you manage to look serious, although you want to laugh.	21
kid	/kɪd/	N-COUNT You can refer to a child as a kid. [INFORMAL]	31
lack	/læk/	V-T/ V-I If you say that someone or something lacks a particular quality or that a particular quality is lacking in them, you mean that they do not have any or enough of it.	27
laughter	/læftər/	N-UNCOUNT Laughter is the sound of people laughing, for example, because they are amused or happy.	21
lawyer	/lɔɪər, lɔyər/	N-COUNT A lawyer is a person who is qualified to advise people about the law and represent them in court.	85
local	/loʊkəl/	ADJ Local means existing in or belonging to the area where you live, or to the area that you are talking about.	23
locals	/loʊkəlz/	N-COUNT The locals are local people.	111
locker	/lɒkər/	N-COUNT A locker is a small metal or wooden cabinet with a lock, where you can put your personal possessions, for example in a school, place of work, or sports club.	31
lonely	/loʊnli/	ADJ Someone who is lonely is unhappy because they are alone or do not have anyone they can talk to.	15
luxury hotel	/lʌkʃəri hoʊtɛl, lʌgzə-/	N-COUNT A luxury hotel is a building where people stay, for example on vacation, paying for their rooms and meals, in very great comfort, especially among beautiful and expensive surroundings.	29
madly	/mædli/	ADV You can use madly to indicate that one person loves another a great deal.	103
major	/meɪdʒər/	V-I If a student at a university or college in the United States majors in a particular subject, that subject is the main one they study.	51
massage	/məsɑʒ/	N-VAR Massage is the action of squeezing and rubbing someone's body, as a way of making them relax or reducing their pain.	29
matchmaker	/mætʃmeɪkər/	N-COUNT A matchmaker is someone who tries to encourage people they know to form a romantic relationship or to get married.	69
mature	/mətyʊər, -tʊər, -tʃʊər/	ADJ If you describe someone as mature, you think that they are fully developed and balanced in their personality and emotional behavior.	107

mission	/mɪʃən/	N-COUNT A mission is an important task that people are given to do, especially one that involves traveling to another country.	115
misunderstanding	/mɪsʌndərstændɪŋ/	N-COUNT You can refer to a disagreement or slight quarrel as a misunderstanding. [FORMAL]	107
Native-American	/neɪtɪv əmɛrɪkən/	N-COUNT Native Americans are people from any of the many groups who were already living in North America before Europeans arrived.	59
navigate	/nævɪgeɪt/	N-VAR When someone navigates a ship or an aircraft somewhere, they decide which course to follow and steer it there.	111
nerd	/nɜrd/	N-COUNT If you say that someone is a nerd, you mean that they are unpopular or boring, especially because they wear unfashionable clothes or show too much interest in computers or science. [INFORMAL, OFFENSIVE]	31
nervous	/nɜrvəs/	ADJ If someone is nervous, they are frightened or worried about something that is happening or might happen, and show this in their behavior.	43
nightclub	/naɪtklʌb/	N-COUNT A nightclub is a place where people go late in the evening to drink and dance.	71
nursing home	/nɜrsɪŋ hoʊm/	N-COUNT A nursing home is a residence for old or sick people.	21
opposite	/ɒpəzɪt/	N-COUNT The opposite of someone or something is the person or thing that is most different from them.	27
outweigh	/aʊtweɪ/	V-T If one thing outweighs another, the first thing is of greater importance, benefit, or significance than the second thing. [FORMAL]	105
overeat	/oʊvərit/	V-I If you say that someone overeats, you mean they eat more than they need to or more than is healthy.	75
overland	/oʊvərlænd/	ADJ An overland journey is made across land rather than by ship or airplane.	111
painkiller	/peɪnkɪlər/	N-COUNT A painkiller is a drug that reduces or stops physical pain.	75
participant	/pɑrtɪsɪpənt/	N-COUNT The participants in an activity are the people who take part in it.	21
part-time	/pɑrt taɪm/	ADJ If someone is a part-time worker or has a part-time job, they work for only part of each day or week.	41
passenger	/pæsɪndʒər/	N-COUNT A passenger in a vehicle such as a bus, boat, or plane is a person who is traveling in it, but who is not driving it or working on it.	99
personal ad	/pɛrsənəl æd/	N-COUNT A personal ad is an advertisement. placed by someone looking for a close friend. [INFORMAL]	69
perspective	/pərspɛktɪv/	N-COUNT A particular perspective is a particular way of thinking about something, especially one that is influenced by your beliefs or experiences.	105
pick up	/pɪk ʌp/	PHRASAL VERB When you pick up someone or something that is waiting to be collected, you go to the place where they are and take them away, often in a car.	99
population	/pɒpyəleɪʃən/	N-UNCOUNT The population of a country or area is all the people who live in it.	79
potential	/pətɛnʃəl/	ADJ You use potential to say that someone or something is capable of developing into the particular kind of person or thing mentioned.	67
pregnant	/prɛgnənt/	ADJ If a woman or female animal is pregnant, she has a baby or babies developing in her body.	57
production	/prədʌktʃən/	N-UNCOUNT Production is the process of manufacturing or growing something in large quantities.	79
psychologist	/saɪkɒlədʒist/	N-COUNT A psychologist is a person who studies the human mind and tries to explain why people behave in the way that they do.	13
qualification	/kwɒlɪfɪkeɪʃən/	N-COUNT Your qualifications are the official documents or titles you have that show your level of education and training.	41
random	/rændəm/	ADJ If you describe events as random, you mean that they do not seem to follow a definite plan or pattern.	77
rare	/rɛər/	ADJ Something that is rare is not common and is therefore interesting or valuable.	13
recently	/risəntli/	ADV If you have done something recently or if something happened recently, it happened only a short time ago.	39
recipe	/rɛsɪpi/	N-SING If you say that something is a recipe for a particular situation, you mean that it is likely to result in that situation.	103
reconsider	/rikənsɪdər/	V-T/V-I If you reconsider a decision or opinion, you think about it and try to decide whether it should be changed.	103

remind	/rɪmaɪnd/	V-T If you say that someone or something reminds you of another person or thing, you mean that they are similar to the other person or thing and that they make you think about them.	71
resent	/rɪzɛnt/	V-T If you resent someone or something, you feel bitter and angry about them.	103
reservation	/rɛzərveɪʃən/	N-COUNT A reservation is an area of land that is kept separate for a particular group of people to live in.	59
respect	/rɪspɛkt/	V-T If you respect someone's wishes, rights, or customs, you avoid doing things that they would dislike or regard as wrong.	39
responsibility	/rɪspɒnsɪbɪlɪti/	N-UNCOUNT If you have responsibility for something or someone, or if they are your responsibility, it is your job or duty to deal with them and to make decisions relating to them.	11
resume	/rɛzʊmeɪ/	N-COUNT Your resume is a brief account of your personal details, your education, and the jobs you have had. You are often asked to send a résumé when you are applying for a job. (mainly AM; in BRIT, usually use curriculum vitae or C.V.)	67
retire	/rɪtaɪər/	V-I When older people retire, they leave their job and usually stop working completely.	23
reward	/rɪwɔrd/	N-COUNT A reward is a sum of money offered to anyone who can give information about lost or stolen property, a missing person, or someone who is wanted by the police.	55
risk	/rɪsk/	V-T If you risk doing something, you do it, even though you know that it might have undesirable consequences.	87
roll	/roʊl/	V-I If you roll somewhere, you move on a surface while lying down, turning your body over and over, so that you are sometimes on your back, sometimes on your side, and sometimes on your front.	87
romantic	/roʊmæntɪk/	ADJ Something that is romantic is beautiful in a way that strongly affects your feelings.	51
salary	/sæləri/	N-VAR A salary is the money that someone earns each month or year from their employer. [BUSINESS]	41
scam	/skæm/	N-COUNT A scam is an illegal trick, usually with the purpose of getting money from people or avoiding paying tax. [INFORMAL]	95
scholarship	/skɒlərʃɪp/	N-COUNT If you get a scholarship to a school or university, your studies are paid for by the school or university or by some other organization.	59
scorn	/skɔrn/	V-T If you scorn something, you refuse to have it or accept it because you think it is not good enough or suitable for you.	111
security	/sɪkyʊərɪti/	N-COUNT A feeling of security is a feeling of being safe and free from worry.	41
selfish	/sɛlfɪʃ/	ADJ If you say that someone is selfish, you mean that he or she cares only about himself or herself, and not about other people.	29
shack	/ʃæk/	N-COUNT A shack is a simple hut built from tin, wood, or other materials.	43
shipwreck	/ʃiprɛk/	V-T PASSIVE If someone is shipwrecked, their ship is destroyed in an accident at sea, but they survive and manage to reach land.	115
shore	/ʃɔr/	N-COUNT The shores or the shore of a sea, lake, or wide river is the land along the edge of it.	83
sign up	/saɪn ʌp/	PHRASAL VERB If you sign up for an organization or if an organization signs you up, you sign a contract officially agreeing to do a job or course of study.	49
silence	/saɪləns/	V-T If someone silences you, they stop you from expressing opinions that they do not agree with.	85
smart	/smɑrt/	ADJ You can describe someone who is clever or intelligent as smart.	97
spam	/spæm/	N-VAR In computing, spam is unwanted email, sent to a large number of people or organizations, usually as advertising.	95
spot	/spɒt/	V-T If you spot something or someone, you notice them.	113
stranger	/streɪndʒər/	N-COUNT A stranger is someone you have never met before.	13

stress	/strɛs/	N-VAR If you feel under stress, you feel worried and tense because of difficulties in your life.	75
surrogate mother	/sɜrəgeɪt mʌðər/	N-COUNT A surrogate mother is a woman who has agreed to give birth to a baby on behalf of another woman.	57
talkative	/tɔkətɪv/	ADJ Someone who is talkative talks a lot.	13
taste	/teɪst/	N-UNCOUNT A person's taste is their choice in the things that they like or buy, for example, their clothes, possessions, or music.	13
tattoo	/tætu/	N-COUNT A tattoo is a design that is drawn on someone's skin using needles to make little holes and filling them with colored dye.	99
team spirit	/tim spɪrɪt/	N-UNCOUNT Team spirit is the feeling of pride and loyalty that exists among the members of a team and that makes them want their team to do well or to be the best.	19
tend	/tɛnd/	V-T If something tends to happen, it usually happens or it often happens.	11
toil	/tɔɪl/	V-T/V-I When people toil, they work very hard doing unpleasant or tiring tasks. [LITERARY]	85
top dollar	/tɒp dɒlər/	PHRASE If someone pays top dollar for something, they pay the highest possible price for it. [INFORMAL]	69
tough	/tʌf/	ADJ A tough person is strong and determined, and can tolerate difficulty or suffering.	15
track	/træk/	V-T To track someone or something means to follow their movements by means of a special device, such as a satellite or radar.	95
trade route	/treɪd rut, treɪd raʊt/	N-COUNT A trade route is a route, often covering long distances, that is used by traders.	115
treat	/trit/	V-T If you treat someone or something in a particular way, you behave toward them or deal with them in that way.	11
trouble	/trʌbəl/	V-T If something troubles you, it makes you feel worried.	43
tuition	/tuɪʃən/	N-UNCOUNT You can use tuition to refer to the amount of money that you have to pay for being taught in a university, college, or private school.	97
twin	/twɪn/	N-COUNT Twins are two people who were born at the same time from the same mother.	57
uncomfortable	/ʌnkʌmftəbəl, –kʌmfərtə– /	ADJ If you are uncomfortable, you are slightly worried or embarrassed, and not relaxed and confident.	39
upset	/ʌpsɛt/	ADJ If you are upset, you are unhappy or disappointed because something bad has happened to you.	15
valuable	/vælyuəbəl/	ADJ Valuable objects are objects that are worth a lot of money.	87
volunteer	/vɒləntɪr/	N-COUNT A volunteer is someone who offers to do a particular task or job without being forced to do it.	13
vote	/voʊt/	V-T/V-I When you vote, you indicate your choice officially at a meeting or in an election, for example, by raising your hand or writing on a piece of paper.	79
working class	/wɜrkɪŋ klæs/	ADJ The working class or the working classes are the group of people in a society who do not own much property, who have low social status, and who do jobs that involve using physical skills rather than intellectual skills.	47
wrinkle	/rɪŋkəl/	N-COUNT Wrinkles are lines that form on someone's face as they grow old.	99
yell	/yɛl/	V-T/ V-I If you yell, you shout loudly, usually because you are excited, angry, or in pain.	27

Reading Strategies Index

Unit 1
Reading 1: Skimming/Making hypotheses (1, 2); Making hypotheses (3, 4); Making judgments (5, 6)
Reading 2: Planning your reading (1); Skimming/Making hypotheses (2, 3); Making hypotheses (4); Making judgments (5); Scanning (6)
Reading 3: Skimming/Making hypotheses (1, 2); Making hypotheses (3, 4); Making judgments (5, 6)

Unit 2
Reading 1: Skimming/Making hypotheses (1); Making hypotheses (2); Making judgments (3); Scanning (4); Making judgments (5)
Reading 2: Planning your reading (1); Skimming/Making hypotheses (2); Making hypotheses (3); Making judgments (4); Scanning (5)
Reading 3: Skimming/Making hypotheses (1); Making hypotheses (2, 3); Making judgments (4); Scanning (5)

Unit 3
Reading 1: Scanning (1, 2); Making judgments (3, 4); Scanning (5)
Reading 2: Planning your reading (1); Making hypotheses (2); Scanning (3); Making judgments (4, 5); Scanning (6)
Reading 3: Scanning (1); Making judgments (3)

Review 1
Reading Strategies Review: Planning your reading (1); Skimming/Making hypotheses (2, 3); Scanning (4)
Comprehension Check: Scanning (1, 2, 3, 5); Deducing meaning of words from context (4)

Unit 4
Reading 1: Skimming/Making hypotheses (1); Making predictions (2–7); Making judgments (8)
Reading 2: Making hypotheses (1); Making predictions (2, 3); Making judgments (4); Scanning (5)
Reading 3: Making hypotheses (1); Making predictions (2); Making judgments (3)

Unit 5
Reading 1: Making hypotheses (1); Making inferences (2, 4–6); Making judgments (3)
Reading 2: Skimming/Making hypotheses (1); Scanning (2); Making judgments (3, 4); Making inferences (5, 6)
Reading 3: Making hypotheses (1); Making inferences (3, 4)

Unit 6
Reading 1: Scanning (1); Interpreting (2); Making judgments (3); Making inferences (4)
Reading 2: Skimming/Making hypotheses (1); Interpreting (2): Making judgments (3)
Reading 3: Skimming (1); Interpreting (2); Making judgments (3)

Review 2
Reading Strategies Review: Planning your reading (1); Making predictions (2); Interpreting (3); Making inferences (4)
Comprehension Check: Deducing meaning of words from context (1, 2); Interpreting (3); Making inferences (4)

Unit 7
Reading 1: Skimming/Making hypotheses (1, 2); Making judgments (3, 4); Making inferences (5)
Reading 2: Making hypotheses (1, 2); Interpreting (3); Making judgments (4, 5)
Reading 3: Scanning (1); Making judgments (2–6)

Unit 8
Reading 1: Making associations (1); Skimming/Making hypotheses (2, 3); Making associations (4); Making judgments (5)
Reading 2: Making predictions (1); Making judgments (2, 3); Making associations (4); Making inferences (5, 6)
Reading 3: Making associations (1, 2, 3); Making judgments (4)

Unit 9
Reading 1: Making associations (1, 2); Skimming/Making hypotheses (3); Making hypotheses (4); Making judgments (5); Deducing meaning of words from context (6); Making judgments (7)
Reading 2: Skimming/Making hypotheses (1); Making hypotheses (2); Making judgments (3); Deducing meaning of words from context (4)
Reading 3: Skimming/Making hypotheses (1, 2); Making judgments (4); Deducing meaning of words from context (5)

Review 3
Reading Strategies Review: Planning your reading (1); Skimming/Making hypotheses (2); Making judgments (3); Making associations (4); Deducing meaning of words from context (5)
Comprehension Check: Deducing meaning of words from context (1, 2); Interpreting (3); Making inferences (4, 5)

Unit 10
Reading 1: Making associations (1, 2); Interpreting (3); Making judgments (4); Visualizing (5); Making judgments (6)
Reading 2: Making associations (1); Visualizing (2, 3); Making judgments (4); Making inferences (5, 6)
Reading 3: Making hypotheses (1, 2); Visualizing (3, 4); Making judgments (5)

Unit 11
Reading 1: Making judgments (1); Summarizing (2, 3), Making judgments (4)
Reading 2: Planning your reading (1); Making hypotheses (2, 3); Making judgments (4, 5); Summarizing (6)
Reading 3: Making judgments (1, 2, 3, 4); Summarizing (5)

Unit 12
Reading 1: Planning your reading (1); Making judgments (2, 4, 5); Scanning (3); Summarizing (6)
Reading 2: Planning your reading (1); Making associations (2, 6); Visualizing (3, 4); Making judgments (5); Making inferences (7)
Reading 3: Planning your reading (1); Scanning (2);

Review 4
Reading Strategies Review: Planning your reading (1, 2); Visualizing (3); Making judgments (4); Summarizing (5)
Comprehension Check: Making inferences (1, 2); Deducing meaning of words from context (3); Interpreting (4); Summarizing (5)